LOVE BEING

WAKING UP

IN THE

NEW CONSCIOUSNESS

Library of Congress Control Number: 2012907826

ISBN: 978-0-9826946-8-8

This book is dedicated to the members of the Visionary Project. Whether you are officially a participant or you are working on your own, welcome and good luck with your Regimens.

Special thanks to Carol Joy for providing her proofreading and editorial expertise to this project.

CONTENTS

Introduction by Mark

Hello everyone. Here we are with our tenth book in our tenth year with Seth. It still seems miraculous, even after a whole decade of collaboration. We are deeply grateful here that Seth has hung-out with us over all these years.

As usual, I will say a few words about the material and then keep quiet while Seth states his case.

First, I think you could also title the book, ***How to Use Positive States of Consciousness to Improve Your Life***. The premise is that as you deal with your Issues and Lessons, you can create these higher states of consciousness. By "living" in these states, you change your reality for the better. But it begins with encouraging catharsis and healing through personalized Regimens. This is what Seth spoke about in ***Resonance***. In this new book, Seth teaches you how to create a Regimen of Love.

Each chapter begins with a Dialogue, a short "chat" between Seth and myself on a topic relevant to the subject matter of that chapter.

Seth told me to stop noting when he is being intentionally funny, so we will not use (Humorously) in this manuscript. He wants to allow the reader to get the humor on their own or perhaps not get it at all. He thinks we were being somewhat pretentious in some of our books by over-using this.

We are including Findings from The Visionary Project. Turn to Page 93 and see how Seth's clients are creating their own Regimens.

That's about it. This is a great book, and a very useful one, for those of you who are eagerly participating in Seth's Teaching. Good luck and have fun.

Introduction by Seth

Welcome. Now let me get directly to the point. We propose to demonstrate a useful system, in which the solitary Practitioner may use Rituals of Love to initiate themselves into an experiencing of the New World or New Consciousness. That is indeed our goal and we will attempt to keep the exercises and experiments focused on that precisely-defined end.

The New Consciousness is inhabited by awakening humans and their non-physical Guides. Here, we take it for granted that the reader is already quite familiar with my works in this awakening matter. You may experience greater rewards if you have worked out the exercises in the previous books beforehand, contacted your Guides, and so on. It makes sense, does it not, to prepare yourself for the task at hand: your personal awakening to your greater reality?

In a similar vein, we are including in this manuscript the Findings from personal Regimens of some of our students. It is our hope that you may turn to these narratives to see how others are doing it. You may notice that each of the participants in the Visionary Project interprets this material in their own way. Also, they must individually apply the material, using "what works," to coin a phrase: using what works best for the individual explorer.

I am very proud of my students who are creating their own Regimens of Reality Creation. This is what it is all about, you see, from my perspective. This is where the magic occurs: in the practice of the techniques and in the experimentation.

Preface

Now please do not misunderstand me. The past books have served their purpose. You have learned the breadth of knowledge regarding this Ancient Wisdom. This is your foundation for the task at hand. All of the Findings you have identified in your past experimentation will assist you in creating Love moment-to-moment. I hope you see what I am driving at here. Your studies over these years were not in vain. They represent the Value Fulfillment of actually DOING. Knowledge becomes wisdom through reading, experimenting, engaging and learning. Then, the <u>application</u> of this accumulated wisdom is achieved, for our purposes, through this simple exercise of embodying Love.

Let us speak in terms of basics to cover, then, in this new book. I believe the Human Virtues, humor, and other initiators of the positive states will be studied. The Sanctuary is intact, you see, as these powerful therapeutics are invoked. This is in the style of the great wonder-workers, magicians, shamans and such, of your perceived past. So we will be revealing their methods in the book. I think it is time to do this. In a sense, it is just IN time that we offer these potent systems of Reality Creation to humanity.

Agreed, this is NOT new information to students of the mainstream and other religious practices. Intentional consciousness change lies at the heart of many of your religions. Here, let me say that we are simply simplifying these practices for the easy implementation of the methods.

PART I

LOVE BEING

(The Microcosm)

CHAPTER ONE

Altared States

Dialogue - This Manuscript

Mark - Shall we plan the book?

Seth - Yes. Now per our discussions, Mark, let us create two sections within this new manuscript: the first section will be titled Love Being, or some such term. In this section we WILL cover the individual and their use of the hedonic practices to create the elementary ecstasy or Good Humor state of consciousness. The other practices to achieve this individualized state of bliss will also be discussed, such as the Virtues of Humanity, and so on.

Then, in the second Part of this book, which we may title Waking Up in the New Consciousness, The Positive Manifestation, or what have you, we shall focus more on the collective. Yes, the effects on the collective of the individual search for ecstasy. Let us not forget our new feelings around the psychedelics and other accouter-

ments. These will be covered, certainly. As well we will continue to mark the development of some of the Essential Metaphors we have been noting in our forecasts and in the new books. In other words, Mark my friend, we will once again attempt to tie-up into a nice little attractive package this Seth Teaching of mine.

Will we succeed? Only time will tell. However, I do sense a distinct probability that this new volume will be quite instrumental in our reaching a far vaster audience than we have until now. This is my hope, as you know: to reach as wide an audience of humans as possible within this current timeframe in which you are experiencing your existence. Am I understood here?

Mark *- Yes Seth. I understand and I support you in these efforts.*

Seth *- Very well then. We begin...*

Word Play

Mark enjoys the pun "altared states," referring to those states of consciousness in which the Practitioner is in direct contact with Source. I also enjoy this term. It has Good Humor attached to it via the similar sounding words altar and alter, and so, may serve as a foundation for the creation of Positive Realities. This word-play has beneficial effects on consciousness, as you know. And I would remind you, as I often do, that ANY moment in your Reality Construction may be identified as an altared state, a Ritualized state of conscious awareness. For you create your reality through your perceptions, essentially, through your perceptions and your focus in the moment.

Thus, I see that the thesis to this Practice as it now stands, may be to first address adequately the Issues and Lessons of creaturehood, as we shall soon describe. Then the student becomes <u>free</u> to Ritually create states of consciousness moment-to-moment, in which Good Humor, Positive Emotion, Love and ecstasy are experienced. Now let us attempt to guide you down this simple path of awakening.

Barriers to Feeling Good

First, I see that many of you are the progeny of a God-fearing people. We have spoken of this before in my books. Your heritage is one of anti-pleasure, primarily. Your religious practices have taught the importance of stern sacrifice. The pleasures of the body were to be avoided, except in the matter of procreation. Briefly, feeling good for its own sake, you might say, was considered selfish and frivolous. Now it was one thing to be exalted in spirit while in prayer to your authoritarian God, but quite another to seek out pleasure because it felt good. So you in this group have a bias, perhaps a subconscious bias, you see, in which your default emotion is to disapprove of pleasure for its own sake, as its own reward.

"Religious conditioning" is the term we have used to describe this limited perception. The human that believes feeling good is shameful or sacrilegious creates a quite limited reality for themselves and their families with this idea. Indeed, you-the-reader may not even be aware of how these idea constructs have limited your exploration of physical reality on your Earth.

Obviously there are other "reasons" for this quite common state, this "fear of pleasure." Trauma and other negative events from the past do indeed color and inform in dramatic ways your current Reality Construction. We will offer solutions to this vexing Issue of the Negative Persona shortly.

Sanctuary

One altared state you may be familiar with as a reader of our little essays, is the state of Sanctuary. It is a beginning state of consciousness that the student practices creating. The Ritual of Sanctuary at the back of our new books, provides some information on how YOU may go about creating your own Ritual. The altared state of Sanctuary is then created, ideally, at the beginning of your day, and then maintained throughout your waking times by continuously seeding your consciousness with the positive thoughts of safety, Loving support and natural ease of expression.

If you are a student of religions, you may recognize the similarities between our Ritual of Sanctuary and the Rituals of spiritual practices worldwide. Ours is a "casting of the circle," essentially, modified to be of use to the modern Practitioner "on the go," as you say. Again, please do individualize your Sanctuary Ritual to meet your specific needs. The more you personalize it and energize it, the more useful it becomes in your world.

The Personal Regimen

The path of awakening to the New Consciousness is also an altared state. We call it the Personal Regimen. It is a collection of personalized Rituals through which the student creates an "opening." This opening occurs when the ego/intellect is allowed to dissipate ever so slightly. When this occurs, the natural state of your human consciousness is invoked. In this state you are in communication via your mental environment with the Divine, the non-physical beings, the Ancestors, your Guides. The veritable secrets of the Universes are there for you to observe and absorb.

However, these openings are brief, at first, and so many who embark upon these voyages give up before the Universes tell them what they wish to hear. In cynicism, often, and in frustration, the neophyte explorer of the Unknown Reality abandons the Quest, the Path of Healing and Enlightenment.

Negative Persona

Indeed, this censoring of the Inner Sense of sight becomes another form of self-sabotage, as you perhaps discover something nasty, something completely unacceptable in the personal underworld. We have called this amalgam of objectionable material the Negative Persona. This aspect of the identity does not compare well, often, with the assumptions you have about yourself. We might say in our books that this Negative Persona then successfully "pushes you off your path." You are pushed off balance, so to speak, and you might abandon the project. You might put this book in the bottom drawer of the desk, and get to it "at another time."

Now... paradoxically, it is <u>through</u> this Negative Persona that you must go to enter the New Consciousness. Through and through you see yourself, then, as you "unpack" all of these elements that make up your Negative Persona.

Objective Observer

This examination of the psyche begins through the Objective Observer's perspective. This aspect of your personal consciousness allows you to witness the Negative Persona without shame, without fear, without anger. You are not drawn back into the repressed material you are examining, in other words. No, you are easily seeing it for what it truly is through this Objective Observer perspective.

At this point in your exploration you are busy documenting your Issues and Lessons. For our purposes, your Issues are what KEEP you from experiencing Love with a capital "L." Your Lessons concern how you go about dealing with your Issues. If you are a fan of denial and intellectualization, for example, you may have, over the years, "stuffed" these embarrassing ideas about self, providing substance for the Negative Persona. Every shameful thought, then, as well as each negative experience has the potential to "find a home" within this shadow self. Now that you are awakening, it is time to face this material and deal with it consciously. Otherwise, it tends to be projected subconsciously into your world where it may cause you problems, and most certainly will impede your awakening.

The Interview

In a light Trance State you approach this material and ask for information. You are embodying the Objective Observer perspective, and so you need not fear the consequences. This Ritual of going-within may take the form of an interview, in which you ask of this Energy Body the specifics of its make-up, including dates of traumatic events, for example, and sensory imagery to flesh out the picture. Give yourself the suggestion that you will remember all of this material when you come out of the Trance State.

Cathartic Release

After you have interviewed the Negative Persona and discovered what is there for you to learn, you make an appointment with yourself. The material in the Negative Persona has healing potential, for it represents the "flip-side" of your public persona or ego/intellect. To be whole, to be empowered, to be awakened, it is necessary to embody this construct Ritually, in a safe environment, so that you may experience the Negative Emotions trapped inside and integrate these lost aspects of Soul with your psyche, what we have called the Essential Identity.

Greatly simplified... as you surrender to the cathartic healing of your Negative Persona, "a light comes on." You are able to see the world clearly. You are no longer projecting your Issues and Lessons onto others. You are no longer seeing through the filters of your personal biases and misperceptions. You take responsibility for your Reality Creation. Love again dawns upon the personal consciousness in this way.

This healing of the psyche occurs during the course of your Regimen. The healing moment may come at any time in your waking world or perhaps even while you sleep. It is the purpose of this Practice to invite to your awareness these denizens of the Unknown Reality. Thus, a successful Regimen in which integration of the Negative Persona with the Essential Identity occurs, may be quite unpleasant, at first. Indeed, it is the witnessing in "the clear light of day," of this charged material - while you are shopping, for example, or while you are speaking with friends - that wakes you up. You awaken quite literally to a greater understanding of yourself and others.

Other Lives

The material may also offer you information on the events occurring in your other lives. This revelation, from my perspective, is the hallmark of your personal and global awakening. You are all receiving specific data regarding your other Reincarnational Existences. For more on this notion, read our book on reincarnational family therapy: ***Soul Mate Soul Family***.

Magical Child

Now enters the Magical Child into this discussion... I trust that you remember our theory of the Magical Child. This altared state is the perspective that you are born with, before socialization, before the impact of negative care-giving, before the experiencing of Negative Emotion. The magical child "sees" the non-physical beings. They experience the extreme pleasure of physical embodiment. They are still in touch with Reincarnational Existences. They are completely absorbed in experiencing Love with a capital "L."

This perspective of Loving innocence IS a magical one, for this child projects Love into its surroundings, and as a Reality Creator, finds their Personal Reality improved, brightened, brought up in frequency. This is the encounter with the Magical Child. This is that perspective that the adult human longs for, you see. The return to innocence is the return to this perspective of experiencing.

We are suggesting that you return to this state for therapeutic purposes, you might say. The Magical Child perspective IS the healing state. It is a perception of Loving Understanding and Courageous experiencing. It is also the key to transforming the Negative Persona and awakening to your innocence, the New World, the New Consciousness, and so on. The adult Practitioner,

10

then, via the Magical Child perspective, creates Rituals of Loving Understanding and Courage to awaken to this Higher-Dimensional environment.

The Non-physical Beings

Now most importantly with regards to this awakening process is your ongoing Trance State. We refer to it as the Uncommon Trance, the one that you co-create with your Source throughout the day. It is indeed the Sanctuary, as well as the meeting-ground for you-the-reader and your Guides. By now, here in our tenth book together, you must have gained some sort of contact with your Energy Personality and/or your other non-physical Guides.

Admittedly, these results of yours may be perceived by you as quite "weak," "incidental," or even "unimportant." Please reconsider these negative assessments if you have them. From my perspective, even a so-called AB-SENCE of positive results, IS a valid Finding. For is it not true that once you identify what does not work for you, that this frees you up to try other Techniques and Strategies that may work for you?

Beyond Doubt

These are not mere semantics we are arguing. Your reality is constructed by YOU in tandem with the forces of creation. The road to encountering your Guides quite naturally LEADS you through your own doubting perceptions. In time you will learn how to manage these perceptions of yours - the Inner Senses - so that you can relish and celebrate even the most microscopic proof of the Higher-Dimensional Beings we call your Guides.

Are you inspired? I hope so. Again, we have given you a multitude of different techniques for tuning-in your Guides. If you are still trying to make that connection, try this simple exercise.

Guided Meditation - Your Guides

You are on a pathway that you have been told leads directly to your Guides. As you walk this beautiful path, you see on the side of the road re-creations of events in your life when you intuitively knew the right choice to make to succeed. The further you walk along this path, the more instances of this simple inner knowing of what to do in your life become apparent. Finally, as you come into a pleasant natural landscape, at a beach, a forest, a hilltop, you recognize that all of those simple instances of intuitive knowing were actually communications with your Source, your Guides. The path to your Source is not complicated. You have been there countless times before, every time you just knew the right thing to do.

CHAPTER TWO

The Lover's Path

Dialogue - Love Light Matrix

Mark - *Seth, could you describe the Love Light Matrix for the readers of our new book?*

Seth - *Yes, we covered that briefly in our 3rd Book. Now this is simply another of our Essential Metaphors. We are building upon our Consciousness Unit theory. Remember, these CU's exist telepathically/holographically at the behest of consciousness. They are fueled by Love, we assert, Love with a capital "L." Thus, as consciousness creates ALL that may be created - All That Is - we also assert that this manifestation activity takes place within a matrix of Coordinate Points. These portals of entry and exit into and from your system modulate the expression of the CU's according to the templates of creation - the Gestalts of Consciousness, remember - the forms of incipient matter representing the all in All That*

Is. The Love Light Matrix is the scaffolding onto which the reality creator fastens their Reality Constructs of all types, including the elements of air, earth, and so on. Everything is aware. Everything is made of CU's. Will that do it?

Mark - *Yes, I think so. Thanks.*

Momentary Awakenings

In this chapter we will focus on creating your Regimen. Now as you know, you are usually in what we call the Common Trance for most of your waking existence. Consumerism, obedience to authority, attention to the status quo, group behavior, and other Gestalts of Consciousness "conspire" to keep you in a strict unaware state, at least for the most part. When you learn to create the Uncommon Trance, however, you begin to have these little awakenings in which you see your created reality for what it truly is. You see your mistakes and successes. In these minute openings you also see your potential for doing much better in this Reality Creation practice.

It is in these brief Moments of Awakening that I suggest you implement some of our methods for extending the awakening into the future. First, however, it is a good idea to personalize these interventions. There are workpages at the end of the chapter, to place your personalized Precepts and other creations.

Tools Techniques Strategies

Create Your Own Precepts

To get a feel for how to personalize these Tools, Techniques and Strategies, and in so doing, make them habitual, please read the following Precepts of the Ancient Wisdom we have covered in our new books. The idea is to attempt to understand the subtext of the statement. What does it really mean to you personally, with regards to this Voyage of Love on which you are embarking? You ask yourself this question. Then you put yourself at the center of this potent idea and re-create it "around" yourself, so to speak. You personalize it, you make it your own, and write it down on the lines below. I think it is best to quickly go through these Precepts and change them without giving it much conscious thought.

Example: *You create your own reality.*

I create Loving realities for myself everywhere I go.

You create your own reality.

_____

You are connected to everything in your world.

_____

You can change the Consensus Reality from your Personal Reality Field.

_____

Emotion is the creative energy of All That Is in action.

Human consciousness is founded in Love.

Diversions from Love through Negative Emotions create Negative Realities.

All imbalances may be corrected through Love and Courage.

You are the sum of your Simultaneous Lives within your current Moment Point.

Your Inner Senses may be used to examine and change anything past, present or future.

You are in telepathic rapport with everything in your world.

Reality Constructs are composed of Consciousness Units of awarized energy.

Coordinate Points permeate matter and space and modulate the activity of the Consciousness Units.

Your Intention, Emotions and Beliefs provide the energy and direction for Reality Creation.

Everything exists initially as Gestalts of Consciousness, the nonphysical templates of creation.

Making It Personal

By "making it personal," what we mean is this: you recite your personalized Precepts to yourself throughout the day, but particularly you keep them in mind when you are enjoying a Momentary Awakening. Thus, you are doing reasonably well, let us say, at "keeping your heart open," as the saying goes, yet you have just stubbed your toe and you are feeling pain. You are off your path for a moment as you perhaps swear at your toe, or what have you, perhaps doing a little dance of pain holding on to your toe. Now the next moment may be a Moment of Awakening for you as you feel a sudden breakthrough of Positive Emotion. Perhaps you are reminded simultaneously of your vulnerability and also your immortality. It may occur to you in a moment of divine bemusement, what we have called a Reincarnational Comedy. This may help you to experience the elementary ecstasy.

Then, it would help you to Embody the elementary ecstasy you are experiencing. Allow it to deepen with your Intent. Walk it around, to see how it feels. Relish it and give thanks.

In the next moment there may be a return to the mundane with an absence of ecstasy. Note it, give thanks, and then physicalize one of your Precepts or even the felt sense, the Feeling-Tone of your perceived ecstasy of earlier. Do you see what I mean?

Resonance Dynamics of Love

We will now describe some other very effective techniques that you may include in your Regimen. Again, you are in your waking world, you have brought your Sanctuary with you and you are attempting to enact your Regimen. You are experiencing incremental results in the Momentary Awakenings. In the next moment, we have suggested, you attempt to extend one of these openings into the future with one of our Resonance Dynamics. I refer you to our book *Resonance - Manifesting Your Heart's Desire* for specifics. Here we will mention some particularly useful strategies you may employ in your attempts to extend a Feeling-Tone of Love with a capital "L" into the future.

These techniques have been modified from their original meanings and purposes we described in *Resonance*. Certainly, however, if these alterations do not serve you in your search for Loving Consciousness, personalize them so that you get the results you require.

Learning/Finishing Up

With this altared state, you acknowledge your Issues and Lessons with Loving humility as though your time on Earth is drawing to a close. Paradoxically, this state has ecstasy attached to it. Have you told those you Love that you Love them?

Remembering/Embodying

With this altared state, you easily remember the Ancient Wisdom Precepts and you Embody them in the search for Loving Understanding and the Courage to attain it.

Wondering/Thriving

With this altared state, you wonder in the Magical Child mode how the New Consciousness will manifest for you in the next moment. As you witness the moment of Loving Appreciation, you express gratitude for all and anticipate more Loving expression in the next moment.

Awakening/Speaking

With this altared state, you identify yourself as a human awakening to Love. You then express this in some form of art or other media expression.

Moment Point/Point of Power

With this altared state, you sense your current moment as a portal to all of your existences. Simultaneously you send out healing messages of Love to all of your lives. Please see the diagram in our book on 911 for more information on this technique.

The Assessing Strategy

Additionally, we suggest you implement these Strategies for Intentional Reality Creation that were first discussed in *Resonance*. I am certain they will be useful to you on your Voyage to the New Consciousness. They are best used when you are assessing how you are doing on your project, your Regimen. As you go about your day, you may find some direction in these strategies.

Three Assessments and Filling In the Blanks

With this altared state of Accessing, you are utilizing a strategy of Reality Creation that has four parts that work successively. The final effort, Filling in the Blanks, you may call "remedial," for you are remedying your current Reality Creation by adding something that is missing, in your personal assessment of the situation. It may seem to be a lot to think about, at first. Over time, however, as you use this strategy, the process becomes automatic.

Now assessing occurs throughout your waking life over the course of the Regimen. You are noticing how things are going for you. As you notice different outcomes of your Regimen, it occurs to you that your results are of a particular type. We say in this Practice that these assessments reveal particular Feeling-Tones. A Feeling-Tone is a perception that has all of the sensing attributes contained within it. In other words, it has imagery, sounds, tactile elements, and so on. It lies somewhere between a memory and a belief, if you follow me. By practicing the assessment of Feeling-Tones in your reality, you begin to wake up to what you are creating. You begin to consciously co-create your world.

Feeling-Tone

An example we have used before: Imagine you have a friend who won a great deal of money gambling. They described the scene to you as they remembered it. Perhaps they told you that "Everything seemed to go in slow motion." That would be a Feeling-Tone with visual and tactile elements. Then they told you that it reminded them of a successful business project. "It made me think I could do anything I wanted to do." That would be a Positive Emotion component of the experience. Then they told you that they remembered a circular thought that used to bring them luck that they would repeat over-and-over to themselves: "I am naturally lucky." This would be a rumination, a positive rumination. Now together, all of these elements combine to make up a Feeling-Tone that represents the sensory signature of the event. You might also say that this Feeling-Tone is the <u>literal</u> foundation upon which this person created their reality of winning. Now the assessing strategy...

Assessing Your Current Feeling-Tone

This assessment occurs when you momentarily awaken from the Common Trance. Your Regimen has been on-going for a few hours, let us say. Still, the tendency is to lapse back into what you might call the "herd mentality." But suppose you keep a small card with you with the word REGIMEN printed on it. Many of my students tell us that this is very helpful. Thus, you take the card out of your pocket, read it, and you are reminded you are on your Regimen. Now is the time to assess your current Feeling-Tone.

Gather through your senses these Findings, as we call them, regarding your Reality Creation in the moment. Please document these perceptions, the sensory stimuli, in a diary or in some other permanent record. Over time, this Practice becomes ingrained and the need to document every tiny perception becomes unnecessary. You become an expert at this, and so you naturally refine the process and do it in your own way and in your own time.

Assessing the Best Case Scenario

This assessment first occurs during a light Trance State. As you relax and consider what you are attempting to create on your Regimen, you let your imagination go to a place in the future in which the ideal outcome of your Regimen is experienced. You know, as a reader of my books, that everything happens that can happen. Everything happens in terms of probable futures, probable realities. So here, you are "peeking-in" on a Probable Future of yours, in which the ideal - the Best Case Scenario - is being experienced.

This perception of the future probable YOU has a Feeling-Tone. Document in some way, after you come to surface awareness, all of the details of this perception of your BCS.

Assessing the Felt Difference

This assessment occurs when you have some time to analyze what is missing from your current Reality Creation. What is it that <u>prevents it</u> from being experienced as the ideal, or the Best Case Scenario? This perception also has a Feeling-Tone of multi-sensory values. Document this felt sense for later comparison.

Filling in the Blanks

Now that you have gathered your Findings on the Felt Difference, on what is missing from your current Reality Construction, you may use this data to Fill in the Blanks. Those positive attributes that are missing from your Reality, you will Ritually project INTO your Personal Reality. Please read the section on Metaphorical Tools for ideas on how you may accomplish this operation of Filling in the Blanks.

The BCS Flowchart

The following chart demonstrates our theorized flow of communication in this Best Case Scenario strategy. You have created your BCS and it now exists as a probable future. Indeed, the probable future YOU that now enjoys the Best Case Scenario is sending back information to you in your current moment. This information is received by you in the form of Impulses to do, think, feel or imagine something. You take Action, for the impulse has ecstatic emotion attached to it. THEN you experience the Insight: the meaning and purpose of the Impulse from your BCS. Insight follows Action follows Impulse.

BCS

v

IMPULSE

v

ACTION

v

INSIGHT

Reactionary Anger

Suppose you are well into your Regimen. Then one day, things are not going well for you and you incur a disagreement with your colleague, friend or Soul Family member. You are having a fight, in other words. Now this is quite the opposite of a perception of Love with a capital "L." Yet please be advised, that this lapse into the negative is inevitable for those of you on this path. The default to anger and fear is common, as you know. And yet, your ARE on your Regimen, and so, suppose again that you have the presence of mind to begin your assessing strategy.

Your current Feeling-Tone might be described as angry and fearful, am I right? This emotional state carries with it the individual sensory values of YOU the Practitioner. I do suggest that the greater part of this material is supported by anger and fear, however. Thus, you might note in your diary the imagery, the circular thoughts, the perceptions of various types you are utilizing to create the lapse into the negative called "anger and fear."

Your BCS regarding the Regimen, might I remind you, is a perception of Love, most likely. Specifically, here, we could say that you are looking for a Loving relationship with The Other. This seems quite simple to me. You are a bit off your path, then.

Immediately, the Felt Difference becomes realized. Here, I would say the Felt Difference is concerned with reactionary anger, as we discuss elsewhere in this manuscript. In other words, the BCS of Love with a capital "L" would contain the ABSENCE of reactionary anger. Then immediately it may come to mind, "What is the opposite of this reactionary anger?" Then the answer may come, "A perception of Loving Understanding and acceptance, ongoing, moment-to-moment, even as I may be provoked into responding with anger and fear, as that is my common personality trait." Do you see how these assessments may meld into each other in the Practice?

Immediately again, having mastered this dynamic somewhat, you infuse your Reality Creation efforts with Loving Understanding and Courage, acceptance, and so on. The resentment has not had time to congeal and create difficulties, let us say. You successfully, through your altered behaviors, words, thoughts in the moment, pull yourself back on the path. The anger and fear are replaced with their opposites. This is the skill of communication that is sharpened during this Regimen.

Enacting Your Regimen

You already know how to do this. Every instance in which you attempted to <u>consciously</u> create your Personal Reality Field with Intent was practice for what you are now attempting to manifest. I further assert that each of these instances of co-creation has a signature Feeling-Tone that contains the essence of the felt instance.

This is my theory, now, yet why not prove it to yourself? Take a miniscule Finding, one of the brief instances in your Practice as an intentional Reality Creator that proved to you that you were on the right track. Feel the power and Positive Emotion of that moment in which you experienced a positive response from your environment, your Personal Reality. Now with that positive feeling in mind, begin to consider how you will proceed. This is your inspiration, you see. Begin there.

Your Choice

Now in this Regimen, your Lessons and Issues are addressed in the moment-to-moment experiencing of your waking reality. Courage and Loving Understanding guide your thoughts and mentality, and most importantly, your <u>reactions</u> to events in your personal world. Specifically, here, remember that you always have a choice in how you react to ANY event. If you react in anger and fear you will slow down this awakening to the New Consciousness. If you react with Courage and Loving Understanding, you will speed up your personal awakening. Again, this may seem obvious to you.

Example: Choosing Love

Your Issue is one of reactionary fear, let us say. You respond to perceived negative events with fear, without thinking, in a sense, "automatically," as you say. But let us suppose you are working on yourself via these Regimens of Intentional Reality Creation. You are thus experiencing subtle changes in your Personal Reality Field: the Third-Dimensional feedback of your consciousness. May we say that for every ten instances of possible negative reactions with fear, you are currently "catching yourself" in a moment of reflection when you <u>choose</u> to respond with Loving Understanding and Courage one-tenth of the time? A small precious Finding, that is what we are describing here. And yet the repercussions of this tiny alteration in behavior Resonate within the individual and collective consciousness.

Techniques From Thought Reality

The following Techniques were presented in *Thought Reality.* Here I have modified them to support the new Regimen of Love we are promoting. I suggest you simply read through these suggested methods, and then focus on those that you would like to personalize and include in your Regimen.

Consecutive Positive Assessments

You interpret your momentary experience in Loving ways. You find the Love in every event in your waking world. That would be your focus.

Distracting the ego/intellect

You easily distract yourself from a focus on the negative to a focus on the positive, or what you might call the Divine, Love, ecstasy. You divert, you distract your attention from fear and anger to Loving Understanding and Courage.

Suspending Disbelief

You anticipate the manifestation of Love in your world, and you encourage it to achieve fullness by endorsing even faint signals that you are succeeding.

Metaphorical Tools

You create helpful etheric devices with your imagination and achieve results by applying them in the real world. For example: How would a Positive Emotion Amplifier work? Now create that with your imagination and use it in your Regimen. This is personalizing in action.

The Box

The Box is a type of Metaphorical Tool, really. Here is how you create The Box...

Imagine a box suspended around your neck, or perhaps suspended in space in front of you, as one of our clients imagines it. When you are confronted with something you do not want to deal with, something of a negative nature, put it in The Box. The Box has the power to transform liabilities into assets, negatives into positives, anger into Love. When you have an intuitive sense that the transformation has taken place, look in The Box and notice what has transpired. You may be pleasantly surprised to find that the contents of The Box have changed.

Love Objects

Now as you know, if you have attended one of our lectures, we often begin these events by handing out what we call "focusing objects" to all of the participants. We have utilized small smooth river stones for this purpose, as well as little toys, marbles, and so on. These are objects that may serve as memory tools for our guests. It is suggested at the beginning of these events, that the essence of the workshop - what the student may value over the next few hours - is captured and contained within the object. Then, our theory goes, when you need to remember what took place that was of importance to you-the-Soul, you retrieve the object, hold it in your hand, focus on it, and so on. The object then releases the information to your consciousness.

Indeed, these objects, because they are used in a Ritual way for specific purposes, hold the charge that you propose, again, going along with our theory. Here, then, as you create your Regimen, we suggest you obtain your own focusing object, one that holds the charge of a state of consciousness called Love with a capital "L," or perhaps one of its antecedents, such as Good Humor, the Virtues of Humanity, and any other positive state that you feel may help you on this Journey to the New Consciousness.

Calling Out

Mark has an object that has this charge and meaning within it. It is a heart cut from a semi-precious stone and then rounded and polished to a high sheen. This works for him. You may find that object that works for you. How may you surmise that the object works for you? It is suggested that these objects "call out" to you, in a sense, asking to be used in these Ritual practices. The object may be a crystal - a highly favored selection by the modern practitioner - or it may be a piece of jewelry, a small branch from a tree, and so on. The important thing to remember, here, I believe, is that the object itself is trying to connect with you.

Animate Universe

This presupposes a belief in the animate universe that I describe in my books. Everything that I have mentioned as possible objects to work with, and indeed, everything that you might consider in your Personal Reality as a suitable object, IS animate, IS alive, IS sentient. That is a given, by now, let us agree on that.

So as you go about your waking reality, as you begin to awaken to the New Consciousness, I suggest that you keep a positive expectation that your Love Object will present itself to you in the normal course of experiencing your world. The object may already be in your possession in some corner of a closet in your home. It may be waiting for you on a hike into the hills, as in a small rock, a leaf, or other product of nature. You may if you wish, use your artistic skills to fashion your piece out of materials of your choosing, and by so doing, imbue it with your personal energy, symbology, meaning.

Charging the Object

After creating or finding your object, you Intentionally put your Love energy into it, using your own Ritual practices you have developed over the course of study with this Seth Teaching. For example: One of our clients has created a small carved Goddess figure that they have fastened onto a metal loop

33

so that they may carry it with them on a key chain. Every time this woman takes out her keys, then, she invokes the Loving energies of the Goddess. This is the idea. This is how you might use your Love Object, and keep it continually charged with your personal energy.

Why does it hold this charge? Because it can, as it is sentient, alive, able to receive and sustain the charge, and so on. It works because you create your own reality. In this way, these Love Objects instantaneously create the altared state you have, in a sense, "programmed" into them. For this reason, it is advised that you find, make, or ask for objects of various types to serve as storage devices for the various states of consciousness you wish to invoke upon this Journey to the New Consciousness.

Element Rituals

Water Rituals of your own making may be highly-effective in creating the individualized state of Sanctuary we are calling the Uncommon Trance. You are mostly water, as you know. This element, as you may also have learned in your esoteric studies, is quite responsive to human thought and emotion. Your Intent, which is simply your personal Will energized by an ongoing connection to your Higher Centers of Awareness, may be used to "charge" water. Again, as you may have charged your Love Objects with the different altared states we are describing in this manuscript, you may also charge water with the energies we are seeking in this Practice.

Now bring a small vial of the water with you into your waking world. When you need to re-initialize your sacred awareness, sprinkle it on your forehead, invoking the energies held within the water, you see.

Baptism

With this in mind, please incorporate the energies of the element of water into your Regimen. For example: Begin your Regimen with a Ritual Baptism, in which you bath or shower with Intent. Your Intent might be directed toward an auspicious beginning of your Regimen. It might be directed toward invoking the divine states of consciousness: compassion, Loving Understanding, Courage, and so on. It becomes an altared state, again, because you are infusing this Ritual behavior with Divine Intent. You are in cooperation with Source, with All That Is.

Personal Empowerment

All of the Essential Metaphors we have offered in our new books are, in fact, simply memory devices. They are elaborate reminders that YOU are the force behind your Reality Creation. You already are the magician, as we have said. These Essential Metaphors, once Embodied, simply give you a context, really, a system through which you may experience your own re-awakened power. I trust that you are receiving the subtext I am attempting to transmit to your consciousness at this time.

Earth Air Fire

Of course you may put to good use the personified energies described throughout your occult practices. There are The Earth, The Air, The Water and The Fire Elements, that we, in this Practice, would call Essential Metaphors. Use them if you wish, along the lines of their originally stated usages in spiritual practice. Or, because you are a creator of your own reality, ascribe your own effects to the use of these Elemental Forces.

Parts of the Practice

We contend that the student may combine and personalize our stated techniques and other elements, to create Ritual for any purpose. For example: In the Ritual perception of Finishing Up, you are attending to your life as though you are about to make your Transition, to expire, you see. This Felt Sense may intimately inform your experiences of loss, such as the deaths of loved-ones, your own eventual Transition, and so on. Indeed, it is my suggestion that if you were at some point today, to write your own Eulogy, that it would be quite informative to your

Soul. It would be healing, from my view. Finishing Up... And so, please re-read and re-employ these techniques to see where they may fit in your Practice to observe and create Commemoration, Eulogy, Baptism, Renewal, Sacred Union, Purification, Prophecy, Strengthening of Resolve, Release, Binding, Personal Power, Romance, Business Success, and so on, as we tell our clients.

How does this fit in with our new paradigm of Love? You are living a life as you create Ritual toward an objective called the New Consciousness. It is via this exalted state that you transcend the mundane world and enter into the new perspective. It is through your mundane life and your experiences that you create the new awareness. Therefore, create your Rituals around improving with Love all of these domains of living that involve you.

The Baseline

You are enacting this Regimen of Love to awaken to a reality in which you are in communication with your Guides: the non-physical beings. Many of you are there now and participating, many of you are making plans to visit, so to speak, and many of you are moving there with high purpose: Determination, you might call it also.

You begin where you are now. I mean that both in terms of the etheric and the physical worlds.

Your Basic Regimen

Create your Regimen using the material we have just discussed. As well, please include your personal Findings from experimentation done previously in your studies with this new material.

Now most of you are divorced from Love. Do not, therefore, be afraid to admit it in your Foundational Statement or in the practice of your Regimen. If you do not have any idea of what Love is, you may count yourself among most of the humans awakening at this time. Now you WILL know it when you see it or sense it. It is unmistakable. It shakes you to your core and invigorates you on all levels. It initiates catharsis within you...

First list your Findings from the Negative Persona interview.

Interview with the Negative Persona:

_____

_____

Next, from your interview material you may be able to uncover what are your Issues and Lessons in this lifetime. This is what holds you back from expressing Love with a capital "L."

Briefly note this material on the lines below.

Issues and Lessons:

_____

_____

Please note instances of healing of Issues that we refer to as cathartic moments. (Example: Unexpected crying or uncontrollable laughing)

The Catharsis:

_____

_____

Now without thinking about it too much, simply write down your main goal in this Regimen.

Foundational Statement:

_____

_____

Describe your search for your Love Object.

Love Object:

_____

_____

Now list the personalized Precepts you will use in your Regimen to help keep you on track to awaken to Love.

Personalized Precepts:

_____

_____

Finally, list all of the Tools, Techniques and Strategies you will utilize in your Regimen.

Tools Techniques Strategies:

_____

_____

Into the Field

Now the Regimen is ready to take into the Field, as you embody the Precepts and utilize the Tools, Techniques and Strategies to create Love with a capital "L." Simply set a date for yourself as to when you will begin to implement your Regimen in your waking existence. Set a timeframe for the experiment in terms of weeks. Many of my students begin with a 28 day period for enacting the Regimen with a couple of days off at the end to create Findings that will be used in the next Regimen.

The following chapters will help you to fine-tune your efforts and keep you on-track with your Regimen.

CHAPTER THREE

Pleasure Principles

Dialogue - Feeling Good

Mark - *When you say that ecstasy is based on the simple emotion of Good Humor, what do you mean?*

Seth - *Mark, you are now enjoying a state of elevated consciousness you might call Good Humor. You are relaxing in your favorite park on a warm spring day. As you look across the lake at your volcano, you <u>add to</u> this already existing good feeling with your positive assessments in the moment. So this next moment is improved, tuned-up, you might say, tuned-up in frequency. Indeed, this personalized expression of your Personal Reality Field feeds back to you, Mark, a quite pleasant "postcard" reality that continues to confirm your positive assessments of these moments. Now indulge me for a moment by attempting to use your Intent to further fuel this representation with Positive Emotion.*

41

Mark - *OK* (I attempted to inject the positive into my reality. MF)

Seth - *Do you see how your positive focus tunes up your reality in frequency?*

Mark - *Yes I do.* (I did feel an improvement. MF)

Seth- *It increases the expression of good feelings, here. You are literally <u>charging</u> your reality with affection and then witnessing the increased ecstasy as you do. Does that make sense?*

Mark - *Yes it does, Seth and thanks for the in-service.*

Seth - *You are welcome, Mark. I <u>am</u> here to serve.*

Seth's Disclaimer

Let me begin this chapter on feeling good with a disclaimer... I am NOT suggesting - nor do I ever - that you avoid, deny or repress Negative Emotions. I AM suggesting that you may consciously stop participating in the continuous re-creation of Negative Emotion. It is a choice, you see. You are given a choice to react automatically with Negative Emotion or to find another way. This other way is the Teaching I offer in my new books.

Now I also believe that even in your moments of Negative Emotion re-creation, it will do you good to inform your consciousness with information from your Source, from your other lives, from All That Is. When this is done, you may, because you have free will, you

42

see, continue with your emotional despairing, if that is what you are doing, yet might I suggest, with the new information informing your consciousness, the catharsis you are experiencing may be quite a bit more therapeutic. End of disclaimer.

The Potential of Love

Getting to Love... You ARE born, quite literally now, from the quiet Good Humor of All That Is. In other words, your Source - what you might think of as the Deity, God, Goddess - does indeed have a "good" sense of humor. Think about what I am telling you here for just a moment. If you are with us in our theory of the Love Light Matrix, and you can sense, perhaps subtly, this Essential Metaphor as the provider of your Earthly reality, does it not make sense, that within this reflection of consciousness exists a precedent for the exalted state of Love? It follows, I think, that the Love comes from somewhere, in the sense that, it exists in different levels of manifestation within this gridwork of 3D Reality.

Look in front of you for evidence of what I am saying. Love exists, that is surely true. Yet as I have often noted in my new books, sometimes it is difficult to find this Love that drives realities. So perhaps we may say that Love with a capital "L" is a potential state of being. It is what we might call a Best Case Scenario in this theory of mine. And surely, though it may be rare in certain contexts of human experiencing - during war, for example - its precedents may be found anywhere you would care to look. Now this is a long-winded explanation of a very simple concept: Love always exists in potential in each of your experienced moments. The way to bring it from potential into actual is to begin with the precedents of Love.

Good Humor and Elementary Ecstasy

These altared states that represent the basic building blocks of Love we have called Good Humor, Elementary Ecstasy, and so on. These states are entries through which, via a proper Ritual approach, the student of consciousness may glimpse the "completed product," so to speak. It <u>is</u> a form of "piercing the veil," when one, either accidentally or Ritually, comprehends Love in its totality.

A simple state of Good Humor, one in which you are simply enjoying your existence by yourself or with another human being, is quite easy to create. You may explore this by attempting to create simple Good Humor through employing your favorite means for relaxing and enjoying yourself. Do you enjoy listening to your favorite music to relax and enjoy the moment? Do you prefer enjoying the sounds of nature, as you relax in a forest or other country setting? Do you like to relax through meditation and the Rituals around that practice of intentional focus? For our purposes in this book, please think about what practices you regularly employ to relax and have a good time. At the end of this chapter, we shall have an experiment in which you may use these practices to create higher forms of Positive Emotion.

Laughter

A simple method you may use to cultivate a state of Good Humor, is to listen to laughter or to watch or listen to a comedy presentation. Laughter is infectious, and so listening to recorded laughter - such as our Laughter Soundscape that we play on our radio show and at our events - quite naturally induces into the consciousness of the listener, a pleasant, relaxed, state of elementary ecstasy.

Transcendental Humor

There is an aspect of this inducement of the Good Humor state that we might call Transcendental Humor. An example of this was given earlier, when our hero stubbed his toe. In the beginning there was pain. Then it dawned upon him the absurdity of his condition. It WAS humorous, sensing himself as a helpless injured animal, perhaps, yet capable of going deeper to experience the existential underpinnings of the event. The sense of comprehension of what you might call "the cosmic joke" enters here. This example, who went from experiencing pain to witnessing himself as the actor in an existential comedy, had transcended the Negative Emotions to appreciate the very Positive Emotion of ecstasy.

The Ecstatic Moment

Now as we have noted in our earlier manuscripts, it is <u>astounding</u> to witness the Divine, All That Is, the ecstatic moment in its totality. To experience yourself within the moment as consciousness creates reality is indeed breathtaking. It is the stuff of the visionary experience that fills the scriptures from your world religions. And throughout history, humans have dedicated themselves to learn from those that know, the proper methods for approaching this encounter, without getting "blown away," as we say, without becoming so disoriented, so afraid, or so excited that they are immediately removed from the exalted experience. The state of consciousness - the altared state of experiencing Love - becomes broken, you see. It falls away when you are ill-equipped to sustain it.

In this way, you might think of this Ritual approach to awakening we are offering you here as training for that moment when you will receive the opportunity to view your reality "head-on," you might say. In other words, after weeks and perhaps months of investigating your personal underworld as well as the various emotional states triggered through catharsis as you face your Issues and learn your Lessons, you will be ably-prepared to view the Divine without restrictions. This is our hope, here, you see. The idea is to provide this training for the solitary Practitioner so that the individual may experience the wonders of creation, just as the adepts of the mystery schools and other spiritual training collectives have done in your histories.

Lightworker Role

For the preceding reasons, it does take, from my perspective, a Lightworker to consciously work within the grid of the Love Light Matrix. Now before you judge me harshly on my choice of terms, let me explain myself as to how this New Age concept pertains to you-the-reader.

You are on a path of Intentional Reality Creation. You are attempting to create your Personal Reality according to very Loving principles. On the surface, then, it appears to others as though you are softening, brightening, becoming sweet and Loving in your mood and behaviors. On an atomic or Consciousness Unit level, however, it is this same process we have often described to you in our books. Your thoughts, your images, your experienced emotions coalesce into Reality Constructs. Your reality is a perception, then, that appears to be changing for the better in this example. It IS a Light Construct, you see. It is a <u>reflection</u> - as in reflection of Light - of your mental activity perceived by yourself and others in your collectives. This is you. This is the reflection of your Essential Identity into the 3rd Dimension, the Love Light Matrix, you see.

Etheric Community

If you follow me, in this metaphor we are describing, the Lightworker uses the Light of creative energy - the CU's - to create Intentionally with Love. Now should you choose to identify yourself in this way, also remember, that you <u>instantaneously</u> become a part of this Lightworker collective. The way to gain access to any collective, in the etheric or in the physical domains, is to lend your supportive energies to these groups. Just as you connect with the Seth Entity by reading my books and doing the exercises, you would connect to this sphere of influence called the Lightworker's Collective by focusing your energies there.

I think this association makes sense for the serious student. It is a logical sequence we are describing here in my works. If you remember in my first book with you since the death of my first collaborator, Jane Roberts, (*911: The Unknown Reality of the World*) I spoke to you in terms of your position within the greater collective of humanity. I spoke in global terms in our first books to hopefully relate to you the critical nature of the times.

Later in the series of books, I spoke to you in terms of the individual, the individual awakening human. We expressed to you the value in exploring your reality as a Scientist of Consciousness. We were attempting to describe this growing movement of humans dedicating themselves to Loving transformation of the planet. Now we see the fruition of these efforts in the Lightworker's Collective: millions of awakening humans comprise this movement now. I think it is appropriate, therefore, to include their efforts in our discussions in these manuscripts. We are all talking about the same thing. We are all describing the use of Light to help and to heal humanity and your Mother Earth.

Chemical Accouterments

We have recently altered our stated position regarding the use of substances - accouterments - to achieve the exalted states. I am now reaffirming my view that with a respectful and studied usage of plant and other revelatory substances, an opening may be found into the personal underworld. Of course, it is up to the student to take advantage of these openings in times other than those in which the substances are active in consciousness, such as during the exercises we offer you in this current manuscript. Indeed, these accouterments are "initiatory substances" when used in this context, that of self-exploration. Use them wisely to awaken, therefore.

Virtues

We primarily speak of two of the virtues of humanity in my new books: These would be Loving Understanding and Courage. Now Courage is required in these Regimens simply because it takes Courage for a Soul to look at themselves amidst their difficult Issues and Lessons. It may be painful. It may be difficult to watch, as in, the re-experiencing of painful events from the past.

Also, it does take great Courage to Love The Other: other human beings, you see, the human beings in front of you. For many of you this is the "deal breaker," to coin a phrase. "Yes," you say to yourself, "this introspection, this self-assessment of Issues and Lessons is good for me. I am being cleansed through this process. But I cannot bring myself to Love a complete stranger, and certainly not someone I do not like or even detest."

Then we speak of Loving Understanding, in particular, as an altared state that must be experienced to be understood. We are speaking of a particular type of Love with this Love with a capital "L." From this perspective of Love, it is imperative that the Practitioner SEE the truth of The Other: the other people in their reality. The student SEES the truth by using an Inner Sense, that "converses" with the Higher Self or Energy Personality of the other person. This is where the Understanding comes in. As you witness the emotional history of The Other, and as you attempt to experience empathy, you do come to a type of Loving Understanding with this human. Unconditional Loving, yes, forgiveness, perhaps. Yet ultimately you do know where this human being - Soul Mate, Soul Family member or stranger - has been and you accept them with Love.

Sexual Ecstasy

Now I am not forgetting the obvious in my exploration of the ecstatic states. Certainly sexual arousal and sexual ecstasy may be appreciated by the student as one of these many doorways to the Divine. Yet, because I am focusing primarily on the solitary Practitioner, I will leave it to you-the-reader to integrate these practices into your Regimen if and as you wish. It is certainly not a requirement, however.

Now for an experiment to end our chapter...

Experiment
Amplifying a State of Good Humor

We will now lead you through an experiment in which you may attempt to extend and amplify a self-generated state of Good Humor. Now first induce a state of Good Humor through any means you would like. A simple method is to use recorded laughter to help you relax and be still and at ease. After you are in your Good Humor state, give yourself the suggestion to deepen this comfortable state of being even further. This is a light Trance State you are entering as you continue to feed your consciousness the suggestions to deepen the relaxation and good feelings. Now just as I asked Mark in our Dialogue in this manuscript to <u>Intentionally</u> build upon the positive feelings, I am asking you-the-student to do the same. Simply <u>Intend</u> to feel the ecstatic emotion come into your awareness. You anticipate this state, you coax it into being, you welcome it, once you realize you are getting results. Sit with this Intention for a few minutes. Play with it, my friend. You are the creator of these states of consciousness.

Findings: Please document your Findings after you come up to surface awareness.

CHAPTER FOUR

Speaker Material

Dialogue - Gods in Disguise

Mark - *Throughout your works you have referred to humans as gods, goddesses, wonder-workers. Why is that so difficult for people to accept?*

Seth - *Simply because you in the US and elsewhere have a collective case of low self-esteem - negative self-assessing, as we call it in the books. Remember, you are taught by your caregivers how to fit in and how to "know your place." Your bosses at the workplace insist that you "toe the line," and behave in a uniform fashion, one like the other, you see. Your religions often teach you the <u>value</u> of modesty and the danger in acting out beyond your role. "Behaving like God is a sin. Only God is God, and He is all-powerful." You are <u>dis</u>-empowered at all steps along the developmental path.*

And here is the irony, the truth that your authorities keep from you, is that your reality is <u>your</u> doing. It is the primary secret of the Universe. You are so powerful that you create the world that you inhabit: your Personal Reality, and also by extension, your collective realities. I will leave it at that and allow the powerful subtext to work upon the consciousness of the reader.

The Speaker Role

Many of you may be familiar with the older works I created with Jane Roberts and her husband Rob. It was in that original material that I first spoke of the Speaker role. The Speaker is simply the human that carries on the tradition of truth-telling in the collective. This truth is the Ancient Wisdom I am speaking about in my newer books. The Speaker, by definition, you see, is compelled in their lifetime to tap into this well of knowledge some call the perennial philosophy, and then tell others about it. Many of you are doing just that, as you awaken to your greater reality in this timeframe.

Now an important part of your awakening, as one of these proposed visionary types we have called the magicians, shamans, witches and healers, the Vanguard, and so on, is to choose your artistic medium and create art to carry on this tradition of Speaking. Essentially, it is your task to create media, art, Ritual from your Findings in your Regimens of Awakening to express your personal vision.

What we call the subtext, the subtext of truth, in this instance, is evident to those who are also awakening at this time. This material serves as a sort of calling card for you to "call-in" members of your Soul Family who are waiting to join you to learn their Lessons with you. If you are lost in this discussion, please catch up by reading my series *The Trilogy.*

Completing Your Work

Your Regimen is complete when you share the essential value of your journey in some sort of expression that others may learn from and enjoy. This completion process, then, becomes one of determining how to best "spread the message" of your discoveries, of your successes, of your Lessons learned.

Giving Up Everything

Now in this manuscript we are asking for you-the-student, after having studied and practiced and perhaps struggled over the implementation of our many suggestions and techniques over the years, to disregard ALL of it. Now I maintain that what has come before stands as a foundation upon which you may build this new perceptual awareness, the Magical Child perspective. So nothing is wasted in this Practice. In a sense, in order to have EVERYTHING you must surrender EVERYTHING. I trust that this conundrum will become understood by you as you create your piece, your presentation of your awakening experience.

Back Engineering

Here is an important part: by imagining you are awakening, you begin to awaken. By planning on how you will tell your story to others on how you awakened, your consciousness begins to make it happen. Do you follow me? You need not wait until you are experiencing what you have read about in books as a "full-fledged" awakening episode before you begin your piece on how you awakened. This is a technique we use in this Teaching that has many names. If you understand the term "back-engineering," go with that as I describe the process, as I believe it applies here...

Your awakening in the New Consciousness is a Best Case Scenario. You are Ritually feeding this probable future of yours with the elements needed to make it a reality. This would be your Regimen. By moving forward with your project even though you may not have experienced an awakening to your satisfaction, according to your criteria, you see, your affirmative expectation that the awakening WILL occur is demonstrated by you in the creation of the project. You will proceed in the creation of the project on information you receive from your Higher Self, your Guides, and so on. This should be fairly easy to grasp by now.

Choose Your Medium

Go to childhood if you are having difficulty deciding what form your Speaker material should take. Conduct the Magical Child Experiment from the end of this chapter. Images, sensations, will arise, reminding you of the varied forms you used as a child to express yourself.

Now obviously you may choose ANY medium you wish to express your Findings in this project. If you have a natural talent for one or the other mediums of expression, use that. If you would like to try something new, use that. The point here is that you are putting your discoveries into a creative form that may be understood by others. You can document this at the end of the chapter.

Begin Your Piece

As you receive Findings in your Regimen, it is a good idea to immediately consider how you may express these truths to others and in what form. Again, this process is one of awakening to your own power of creation: the power to create your world the way you would like it to be. Simply, by creating a piece, or a dance, or a text that holds within it the essence of the truth you have discovered, you are making physical, you are embodying, you are manifesting into the Third Dimension these etheric concepts. It is one thing, you might say, to tell a friend or family member in gasping jumbled narrative what you have discovered. It is quite another to show them your piece or your performance, and allow them to experience the essence, the subtext of the awakening experience. Now you will have to learn this on your own: Learning by doing. Anticipating the insight following the action. This is how it always will be for you as a human living in the sequential time space.

Sharing with Others

If you begin to create your project before you have had your complete awakening, as you see it, it is entirely appropriate to share the important Findings that you have made with others. As I have said, you will attract Soul Family participants in this way. These relationships Resonate into being as you, in a sense, go about intuitively putting together your presentation. Because this is true, you may well find that the people that come into your life "coincidentally," through sharing your discoveries in this way, quite naturally become incorporated into the project itself. This may seem outrageous to some of you reading this, however, please be assured that the assemblage of Soul Families in the varied incarnations is done on the etheric level first, just as we are describing.

Your Project

Briefly describe your project on the lines below. This is simply to give you an outline as to how to proceed. If you are creating your project without having had the awakening experience to your satisfaction, please observe how this attention to the creation of your project helps you to Fill in the Blanks. I am not being coy here. This technique will help you to wake up if you have not had perceived "successful" awakening experiences. I will leave it at that. Now the outline.

Title of the Piece:

_____

Medium of Expression:

_____

Notes:

_____

_____

_____

_____

_____

Experiment
Contacting the Magical Child

The key to contacting the Magical Child is imagination. On the premise that you create your reality out of your imagination, tempered by belief and expectation, in this experiment we will attempt to keep contrary beliefs at bay. Now create your light Trance State. Breathe rhythmically. Focus on the stillness within your consciousness. Consider your Findings as to what the Magical Child perspective is for your personally. Does it relate to a time in your life, an incident in childhood? Often there is this boundary between the life lived as the Magical Child and the beginning of the adult life. Find that boundary in your Emotional Body as you understand it. Now cross that boundary from your current adult perspective into the Magical Child perspective. Remember, your imagination now gives you immediate results. Attend, therefore, to what you truly desire. Receive the information that the Magical Child wishes to tell you. Make an appointment to meet with this aspect of your identity at another time. Slowly come back to surface awareness.

Findings: Document your Findings.

PART II

THE NEW CONSCIOUSNESS

(The Macrocosm)

CHAPTER FIVE

Awakening Earth

Dialogue - Signs of Waking Up

Mark - *Seth, could you describe some signs of awakening for our readers? I still get messages from people who refuse to believe that anything unusual is happening.*

Seth - *First, let me express my condolences to the deniers you are hearing from at this time. Monumental changes are in force within your system. It takes a quite dense and impenetrable barrier of denial and intellectuality to sustain this perspective that insists nothing unusual is occurring. So this is sad. We may feel sorry for these Souls. Please note that I am having fun here...*

Now the signs. A moment...

Let me relate these signals from consciousness that transformation is occurring on a grand scale, to events everyone is experiencing, the deniers as well as the awakening ones and everyone else .

You ALL are "swimming" currently, in a psychic sense. You ALL have lost your moorings, to a degree, and you are plunged into chaos.

The perception of time - perceived time - is speeding up. It is a palpable change in time, as it is experienced by the average human.

A perception of "instant manifestation" - what you hope for, dream for, imagine and pray for is becoming sooner rather than later, now.

God, Goddess, Spirit, is now pervasive. This is your collective awakening spirit "looking in" on itself.

I will stop now and ask you to prove to yourself that this is true. Also see how this state of affairs may frighten some people into denial and the search for "rational" explanations.

Counterparts Throughout Time

An expansion of consciousness is occurring for you that is a natural outgrowth of your Personal Regimen. The personal becomes the global, you see. Through a type of "psychic outreach" you will link-up with others of your persuasion. These are humans, such as yourself, who value the

Spirit, who courageously explore their psyches and the collective consciousness, who are dedicated to changing themselves and the Earth in positive life-affirming ways. These meetings occur spontaneously, synchronistically, magically in your Personal Reality. This includes your online world, and all instances of collective effort: political campaigns, groups at the workplace, and so on.

We first spoke of this in our second book together since my return, *The Next Chapter in the Evolution of the Soul*. In that manuscript I reminded you of your counterparts. These humans are connected to you via Soul Family relationships throughout time: past, present, and future. We have stated that you have a form of "contractual obligation" to meet with these humans, to work out your Issues and learn the Lessons of physical existence.

Coincidental Meetings

It does add a whole new level of learning and appreciation to your life when you consider the truth of what I am telling you here. Thus, the "coincidental" meeting with a stranger on the street or in the market place, who, as it turns out, appears to be a person with many of your interests and proclivities. They appear to you as being perhaps a relative of some kind. Yet this is impossible, as you find out. This person is not related to you, at least not in the common sense. They ARE related to you throughout time, however, in the <u>un</u>common sense. They are a counterpart of your Soul Collective, you see. They are entering your life to teach you something and to learn something themselves. They always do this in all of your lives. You are always meeting each other and you are always being astounded at your similarities in personality and temperament and in how the meetings occur.

That is all I will reveal at this time concerning your counterparts. It is up to you to make these discoveries for yourself. There is a brief Experiment at the end of this chapter to help guide you on your way to these reunions.

Microcosm to Macrocosm

In my Forecast for 2012 I noted for the reader several trends and potentials that have a high probability of manifesting in the next few years. You may use this information to your advantage as you wake up in the New Consciousness. At the risk of repeating myself, it is YOUR Loving thoughts, images, emotions, and so on, that create a potential for the New Consciousness to manifest. Your focus on these probable future manifestations energizes them and supports their inevitable creation in your world.

These trends and potentials are powerful cyclical movements afoot within the individual and the collective consciousness. Let me now utilize this material to help shed some light on how the individual search for ecstasy, Love, virtue contributes to the collective manifestation.

Ancient Wisdom - Personal Empowerment

As the Ancient Wisdom is remembered, the individual is empowered. Then, as you remember that you are the creator of your world, and that you are compelled to create through Love with a capital "L," you may feel a sense of empowerment in that recognition. You are recognizing your god-self: that aspect of your Essential Identity that KNOWS you are immortal, that sees the particulars within your other Simultaneous Lives and observes with Loving compassion as you make your Transition at the end of those lives.

The Shift - A Cycle of Renewal

The Shift in Consciousness is a naturally occurring, though infrequent, expression of All That Is in the 3rd Dimension. Again, the emphasis is on Love as the basis of all realities. The mundane status quo reality is renewed as "the things that really matter" once again become the focus of millions of people. It is as natural as falling rain or sunlight.

Changing of the Guard - The Visionary Leader

In this cyclical fashion, the Negative Leaders are being evicted from their places of power by the average citizen. The rise of the Visionary Leader perspective empowers everyone to lead by example. You, for example, on this path of Love, are demonstrating to yourself and to others that it can be done and that humanity is healed by the individual healing themselves.

Secrets Revealed - Healing the Past

The past is healed and the individual and collective consciousness is renewed. Shameful memories come to mind to be healed and the negative efforts of authorities and leaders to control and harm others are revealed to all. In this manuscript, we might say that your Negative Persona becomes your vehicle for transformation. As you heal your secrets, you are awakened. As the collective heals their secrets, the world is awakened.

Goddess Rediscovered - GA Remembered

Memories of the lives lived in the Divine Matriarchy inspire the individual to reject authoritarian, patriarchal practices. New religions are created according to the principle of The Divine Feminine. This may serve you as you consider the scope and power of these transformations. The Goddess re-discovered IS a return to Love. GA remembered IS a bleedthrough to the ancient matriarchy that was based on Love of The Other. With this in mind, you could say that your personal Regimen of Love has the momentum of these Divine Returns behind it. For practical purposes, you could say that you experience less resistance than before as you attempt to lead a Loving Courageous existence.

Expecting the Worst - Anticipating the Positive

As the Negative Media lose credibility, it becomes easier for the common citizen to anticipate a positive future rather than a negative outcome. For you, as you walk your path of Love, the Negative Media is over-looked as you seek-out only the positive, the Loving in physical reality. Again, you are working with the natural cyclical forces as you look forward to an awakening in the New Consciousness.

Isolationist - Neotribal Collective

You have been kept divided so that you may be easily controlled. As you awaken, memories of tribal existence in other lifetimes prompt you to join together with others of like mind and spirit. In other words, your Regimen begins on the solitary path and yet it is sustained in the collective. You will naturally wish to ask others how they accomplished their goals, just as you will reveal the particulars of how you awakened.

Thinking Globally Acting Locally

Fine-tuning your Regimen for the collective entails "thinking globally while acting locally." You are connected to all of humanity through the Consciousness Units that make-up you and everyone and everything else in your reality.

The key here is to Embody this concept, this Precept as we call it, with such determination and skill that you begin to quite naturally anticipate your positive behaviors, emotions and imagery appearing within the collective manifestation. Through this process, your every moment in waking reality becomes an altared state, for you are consciously co-creating with the collective consciousness All That Is, your Personal Reality. Simultaneously, then, you anticipate, endorse, and, indeed, CAUSE to exhibit your piece of the manifestation within the greater collectives of your world: family, neighborhood, city, state, nation and world. I realize this idea may completely stretch your capacities of comprehension to their limits, yet this is the way it is done. This is what you do now as a Lightworker, one who serves Humanity and Mother Earth with Love.

Experiment
The Counterpart Encounter

You might want to make this experiment a part of your on-going Regimen. Basically, it is a simple affirmative expectation that you WILL begin to meet your human counterparts as you go about your waking reality. Obviously there is this assumption that you BELIEVE it is possible. This comes first in all matters of Reality Creation. The belief, you see, is the foundation for the creative act, the created reality.

This belief may be stated in this way: "I fully expect to meet with my Soul counterparts. I am open to these meetings and I invite these Souls into my world." Naturally you would use your own terminology and so forth to create your personalized affirmative expectation. Then, when you have created it as best you can, you "entertain" that vital concept as you go about your life.

Often what occurs next is a series of signals you receive in the form of synchronicities and deja vu experiences. People who appear to be very much like you or complementary to you begin to show up in your reality. You may read about them in the newspaper. You may see them on the television. Then, they begin to show up in your life in a very unusual fashion. It is unusual because you were "just thinking that thought," you see. It is a co-incidence, a synchronicity because you were "just wondering about how these meetings would occur." And then the meetings occur.

Soul Family contractual obligations are kept in just this way. It is only in hindsight, long after your Soul Family member has been brought into the family, that you realize how extraordinary the association is and how unusual and odd was the initial meeting.

Findings: Document your Findings.

CHAPTER SIX

The Collective Good

Dialogue - THGFAC

Mark - *In our books you have spoken of the value in Thinking Globally and Acting Locally. Does this relate to the concept of The Highest Good for All Concerned? It seems to.*

Seth - *Yes, these concepts are directly related, in my view. The binding unit, so to speak, is our Consciousness Unit. Now we suggest that the ethical Reality Creator Intentionally create their individual realities for The Highest Good for All Concerned. This includes the Reality Creator, obviously, and everyone else, all of humanity. All are endorsed in this view.*

You, Mark, are connected to all of humanity via the CU's of which you are composed. As you, for example, project with your Intent, while you are feeding your birds, for example, that ALL of humanity, all of creation, you see, is sustained, nourished, fed, you ARE acting locally - within your Personal Reality Field. Yet your field is attached to all fields, as All That Is is composed of the telepathic/holographic CU's. Thus, you are quite effectively doing your part to nourish All That Is, even as you go about the simple task of feeding your bird friends in your own little part of the world. The Intent, the motivation, the state of consciousness is important, here. You are not allowing cynicism, fear, anger, Lack or any other Negative Emotion to cloud your vision. You ARE the magician, the shaman, the witch in this moment, this collective moment with everything that exists, including your very well-fed birds, Mark. Do you see?

Mark - Yes Seth. Thanks. I think I see it more clearly now.

Seth - I will accept your thanks on behalf of everything that exists.

The Visionary Leader

Now the collective good begins with the individual, in our theory. We are about to begin a book on the subject, but let me now offer you some of this information here, so that you may use it in your Regimen of Awakening. We have referred to the individual role of leader within the collective as the Visionary Leader role. This person is awakening to their higher self, in the sense that, they are consciously co-creating their existence with their Higher Centers of Awareness, or through Spirit, if you prefer. You may know some of these personality types. You may be one of them yourself.

The Role

Briefly, the Visionary Leader leads <u>by example</u>. They lead themselves, first, you see, by aspiring to behave, to think, to emote for the highest good of all: for the highest ideals, and so on, to which humans of the collective may aspire. These people offer themselves as role-models, in the sense that, their virtuous behaviors invite others in the collective to emulate them. They <u>are</u> charismatic, quite often, as they are simultaneously empowered, awakened, and yet also humble. These personality traits are quite attractive to others. Naturally others try to emulate what they see as these beneficial attributes. Then, in time, the Visionary Leader inspires a following of other humans who are also leading their lives along these high principles. The collective, then, is not "led" in the modern sense of that term. The collective leads ITSELF. Everyone is going in the same direction, you see, not out of the herd instinct, so-called, but out of a telepathic rapport within the group that binds one to the other out of mutual preferences, personality characteristics, perceived goals, and so on.

Defer to the Highest Good

Now supporting this expression of the individual Visionary Leader, is a "tendency" of personality that lends a cohesiveness to the group. When differences are noted by individuals within the group, differences that may have, at other times, under other circumstances, caused anger, resistance, judgement, and so on, these negative influences within consciousness are surrendered altruistically, for the continuing highest good of the individual and the group. Thus, for altruistic purposes, ego/intellect Issues are not allowed to cause problems within the group as a whole. These elements of consciousness are "sacrificed," in a sense, for a common purpose: to allow the group to thrive.

This is Ancient Wisdom material. Originally, in some of your ancient civilizations, it was unspoken and automatic, this deference to the positive development of the group. Now that this aspect of consciousness is coming up again to be recognized and utilized, I sense that it will be used consciously at first, and then as the collective masters this practice, these dynamics of consciousness will become automatic. The highest good for all concerned will be the unspoken motto of your future global civilization. Again, what you desire personally, as ego wants, is given up if it conflicts with what is the highest good for the group.

Experiment
The Visionary Day

This experiment entails Embodying the role of the Visionary Leader for a full day. Remember, this empowered perspective creates reality for the highest good for all concerned. This person models the ethical existence for others, and leads in this way. Now this experiment may be quite pleasant for you, if you may imagine yourself playing this role of Visionary Leader as an actor would, in that, you may always return to your own character at the end of the day, just as any actor does.

Have fun with this experiment in role-playing and don't take it too seriously. It is suggested you begin your experiment as soon as you rise for the day after sleep. Prepare for this day in advance by placing reminders throughout your home, for example, signs, that you are to be a Visionary Leader as well as you possibly can, that you will continuously defer, moment-to-moment, to the perceived highest good for all in your collectives. These collectives would include, your Soul Mate relationship, your Soul Family, your work collective, and so on.

Now additionally, please note that this is a very pleasant existence, this life of the Visionary Leader. It feels good, ecstatic, really, to lead your life in this ethical fashion. Use then this positive feedback of pleasant feeling to continue your role-playing exercise for the complete day if possible.

As in any other of the Regimens you may initiate, keep notes or otherwise document your exploits over time. Even the mundane noting of happenstance events during this day, may, at a later date, yield Findings, as in synchronicities, Impulses from your progressed reality, and so on.

Findings: Document your Findings.

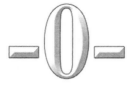

CHAPTER SEVEN

Ecstasy Synergy

Dialogue - Collective Will

Mark - *You refer to the empowered will of individual humans as Intent with a capital I, or Divine Will, if there is a spiritual awareness. How does this Intent or Divine Will work within the collective?*

Seth - *Resonance, Mark, Resonance is created on a grand scale within the manifestation activities of collectives. In the Resonance phenomenon, as you know, synergy is created, such that, the energy created is greater than the sum of the energies projected by the participants. This unusual factor is key in the manifestation projects of collectives. In other words, it becomes easier to create something the greater the number of inspired humans participating. For example, great numbers of worshippers combine their manifesting energies toward collective goals. These collectives are in Resonance with a capital "R," as we call it. Ideally, they are doing* *"good works." They receive what they ask for en masse, just as the individual manifestor gets what THEY ask for, in terms of conscious or unconscious creation.*

Mark - *By unconscious collective creation, are you referring to the exploits of some nations in which they create war with "God on their side?"*

Seth - *Yes Mark. The subconscious manifestation of large groups of worshippers may support war and other atrocities. The collective subconscious holds repressed fear, anger and other Negative Emotions and potentials. Historically, some of your religions have used this dynamic to rally their constituents in wars against other nations. We would call this resonance with a small "r." As well we would describe the ongoing disputes that individuals have with their neighbors, for example, as resonance. This is low frequency resonance, as it is based on Negative Emotion. Do you get my meaning Mark?*

Mark - *OK . Yes I do. This time it's personal?*

Seth - *Yes Mark. Love thy neighbor as thyself.*

Group Power

The individual's search for Positive Emotion finds expression in the spiritual collective. As I have remarked elsewhere, there is a Generalist Spirituality that is making itself known within the collective consciousness. It has elements of the Divine Feminine at its base, but it is non-denominational in the extreme, in that, no individual participant may define what the movement in fact is and what it represents. Again, this reflects, does it not, the perspective of the Visionary Leader, of the awakening one, that sees no hierarchy of power within any group but merely equals everywhere? Do you see what I mean?

Generalist Spirituality is a personalized path of awakening, quite similar to what we are offering to you in our new books. It has neotribal influences, of course, as I have stated in my last few manuscripts. It has an aspect of anarchy to the uninitiated eye. Yet this collective is organized around the key principles we have covered here. It is a self-directive autonomous unit, this collective, that is powerful because there IS no hierarchy of power within the group. The individual participants have taken BACK their power from authority figures. They are now em-powered, thereby. The individuals and the collective are powered by Love with a capital "L."

Synergy

Additionally there is this added effect, one that you may call "synergetic," and by this I mean, the utility and efficiency of always having deferred to the highest good, in a sense, "harvests" energy in the exercise. The collective energy is thus enlarged to greater than the sum of the individuals involved. Put another way, the electro-magnetic expression of the group is "tuned-up" and brought into balance, in a way that is very noticeable to the observer. You needn't take my word for this. Go to any gathering of the Generalist Spirituality movement and you will get a sense of what I am suggesting here.

The Momentum of War

Now referring to our Dialogue for this chapter, please consider what might be the outcome of the concerted efforts of a collective, such as the USA, if these efforts were re-directed in a positive way: from the pursuit of war in many countries of the world, to a pursuit of peace and prosperity throughout the world. To use our vernacular, the resonance with a small "r" that facilitates the creation of negative realities, would transform into Resonance with a capital "R."

Let me also add that the synergetic effect is operative in BOTH CASES. That is why, even though the majority of your citizens in the USA have expressed their distaste for war, that the horrible momentum of this collective manifestation remains so strong. True, it is changing for the better as many of you awaken and challenge the status quo. Yet to break this momentum, this inertia of perceived value in conquering other nations, takes the concerted efforts of millions of Lightworkers and other Lovers of humanity and Mother Earth.

I do see the tipping point approaching for this radical transformation. That is why we are creating our inspirational texts at this time: to help steer the collective consciousness, including the collective Intent, toward peace rather than conflict, towards Love rather than hate or fear.

Experiment
Meditation on Love as World Healer

In our experiment, we will attempt to cultivate within the individual consciousness, a focus on Love with a capital "L," to such a degree, that we can easily imagine this Loving energy moving out into the collective sphere of Reality Creation to influence the manifestation of humanity and Mother Earth. We do this as we always have done this: it begins with a turning inward, toward the stillness that lies at the base of consciousness. At this time, it may be quite easy to accomplish the Trance State. This relaxing state is marked by coolness rather than heat, patience rather than anxiety, Courage rather than fear. As you Embody these sensations ideas and images, a state of Good Humor is naturally achieved.

This is quite easy to do, then.

Having achieved this very satisfying state of being, it is natural to imagine this focused state of stillness, peace and happiness radiating out from you. You are connected to ALL of Humanity and Mother Earth through your common elements. You are able, then, to impart to the macrocosm your Feeling-Tone of Loving Understanding and Courage that you are now manifesting. This is instantaneous, this transfer of energies between YOU and everything else. You can FEEL this energy as it is transmitted to the whole, as it is transmitted to particular areas in the world that need it, as it is sent to friends or Soul Family members either near or far who need it. You are not diminished, you are energized and empowered by this sharing of energies. As you return to surface awareness you are quite able to maintain the power and urgency of this experiment.

Findings: Please document your Findings after you come up to surface awareness.

CHAPTER EIGHT

Global Community Organizing

Dialogue - Extended Soul Families

Mark - *In our second book together you described the power inherent in "your single loving thought." Could you explain how that works in groups of various sizes?*

Seth - *I will take you literally, here. Now, in the relationship we call the Soul Mate collective in our books, for example, your single Loving thought becomes quite powerful when you and your partner are on the verge of engaging in a conflict, a fight of some sort. It takes two angry humans to create a conflict. Also, do you see how it is, that, if one of the partners were to embody the <u>opposite</u> of the emotional state of anger, right at the last minute, <u>before</u> sliding into the inevitable conflict, that the collective mood or emotional environment of the participants would change? Try it. It is good practice. For it is on this basic level of relationship with The Other, that* *one LEARNS how to create Love in the moment. It is a choice, is it not, a choice to abstain from habitual negative Reality Creation, and to, instead, embody Love with a capital "L?"*

Mark - *Interesting.*

Seth - *Now on these other levels of relationship with The Other, such as, at the workplace, within groups of whatever size, you see, simply extrapolate in your imagination and "see for yourself" how the interjection of Love by the individual changes the entire paradigm, re-gardless of the size of the collective.*

Mark - *Regardless of size?*

Seth - *Now Mark, remember the CU's and synergy?*

Mark - *OK Thank you for the explanation.*

Seth - *You are welcome.*

Love is the Answer

When you defer to Love in all of your relationships, in all of your actions - even on your Internet, even on the phone - you are softening, you are soothing, you are making right the energies within those collectives, big and small. This may be your Intent, as I see it, as this Lover of Humanity and Mother Earth. It may be thought of as your job description in this new role of yours as Lightworker, if you accept that designation, as you enact your Regimens of Love in physical reality.

It is potent, then, this active ingredient of Love. It is not diluted in the collective, it is potentiated in these groups. It is the magic ingredient. Now this is the message, also, of your great religions. Love is the answer to all questions. Love is the healer of all wounds. These messages of Love from your spiritual traditions are powerful and Resonate <u>because</u> they are quite true.

Basic Spirituality

As we have noted earlier, these efforts of ours support the creation of a Generalist Spirituality. We are offering a particular assortment of Spirit technologies that the interested reader my employ to create THEIR OWN Practice. We see this as honoring a return to the basics in this matter of Reality Co-creation. However, please change this information to suit your inclinations when and however you wish. Being the basics, they INVITE elaboration, embellishment, personalization, as we say.

And as we leave you to your experiments on the Path of Love, we ask that you study the Findings of our Visionary Project participants that appear directly after the Experiment at the end of this chapter. A quick reading of this material will provide a starting point for you and your Practice as well as ongoing support and inspiration.

Experiment
Anticipating the Global Awakening

Our final experiment is an extension of the ***Look into a Stranger's Eyes*** exercise from our first book. It is a logical extension according to our theory on the nature of consciousness. Let me go on... As humanity awakens, it becomes obvious in the eyes. As you look into the eyes of your fellow humans, therefore, you begin to see these signs of mass awakening. There is a clarity and a kind energy that you may sense in the eyes of an awakening human. This energy is noticeable to the degree that it is there within that particular consciousness.

Thus, as you go about your waking reality, with these ideas of a Global Awakening in mind, look for the signs of kindness, of energy - what you might call Loving manifestation energy - coming out of the eyes of the members of your various collectives. Now of course, these effects are noticeable in your own eyes, Look for these beneficial signals from consciousness, therefore, when you are looking for your own proof that what I am telling you is true.

Findings: Document your Findings.

Epilogue

This ends our book on the creation of the Regimen of Love. Now it is up to you the explorer of consciousness to Courageously move forward with your plans for creating Loving realities. Please note that this is an ongoing learning process for the researcher. Results that impress may come quickly, yet, for most, we are finding, results are small in the beginning. Look for these effects, then, and document them. Be inspired and appreciative of the signals from your Unknown Reality. It is in these small details of living the Regimen that you will create a rhythm, a noble sense of purpose, over time.

Thank you for participating and we look forward to discussing other subjects of interest with you in our next manuscript.

THE

VISIONARY

PROJECT

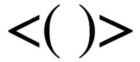

Seth's Letter to Participants

The Visionary Project, as I see it, will be an Independent Study class for students who are familiar with my new messages and wish to take this Teaching of mine further. We are selecting students from different countries so that the data we receive will have a broad context, as in the awakening of humanity, you see. We will begin with students from five countries: the USA, Great Britain, Italy, New Zealand and Germany. (As it turned out, our client in Great Britain dropped out at the last minute. MF) *This will form our core group, then, as Mark understands it. Over time, I envision that students of other countries will engage in this discussion in the Visionary Project...*

I see that we will have phone conversations, radio show instructions, and e-mail communications to support these efforts, so please have these conveniences at your disposal. The first class will be brief, lasting 28 days. The instruction will be ongoing, as in, during both the waking and sleeping states. We will build a dream class to complement the physical class, in other words, just as I have done with Jane and her students decades ago...

I think that will be it for now. I do see the coming class and classes as providing a deep enrichment of the living experience for those of you who take up this challenge. Goodbye for now.

Mark's Letter to Participants

The class begins within the next two weeks whenever it is convenient for you, and ends 28 days after that date. This will be a Regimen, so the practice of the techniques and strategies Seth talks about in his new books should be ongoing for the full 28 day program.

It is suggested that students be familiar with the material in Seth's new books. It is from this material that you are asked to select what practices and techniques you want to implement in creating what you want.

The goal of the class is your creation. It can be whatever you want it to be. Lately I am finding that Seth's phone clients are interested in Lessons, healing, Soul Mates, and abundance, primarily. These are good examples of what students can work on. We would like a brief description of your Regimen... Please refer to Thought Reality and his other experiential volumes for ideas on how to create a Regimen.

Seth does want to include your Findings in the next book. Ten pages will be devoted to each student who chooses to participate...

General guidance via The Seth Frequency Radio Show. The material will be focused on The Visionary Project in a general way. No names will be used....

The Seth Frequency Radio Shows over the next two months will focus on the creation of the new book. The new book is based upon the other books Seth has written with us. Once again, he is distilling his message, simplifying it...

The first half of the book will focus on achieving Good humor, ecstasy, Love to awaken on the microcosmic level. The second half will describe how to participate in creating the collective Positive Manifestation on the macrocosmic level. Individual and collective awakening are the goals, just as he described in his first book with us *911: The Unknown Reality of the World*.

Ann in the USA

I have just finished reading through the written record of my 28 day Regimen with The Visionary Project – recounts of dreams, daily journal entries, notes of feeling tones and incoming information. Wow. I am smiling. This is a big and powerful experience.

My stated goal for the project was to awaken. I wrote to Seth and Mark, in part

"My goal for The Visionary Project is to awaken. It is my deepest longing to know my true nature in all its dimensions, to be at ease in this world feeling my groundedness in a greater reality and to use my personal power to benefit life."

I am only now beginning to get a sense of the magnitude of this desire and the adventure of the journey towards its fulfillment.

I was given the initial instruction to read something from one of the recent Seth books before going to sleep and to ask to participate in and remember my participation in a dream classroom. Although I remembered many dreams, I never had a dream experience of being in a literal class-room. I would imagine myself in a classroom with the other nine participants in the project and Seth as the in-structor during waking hours, however, and I enjoyed imagining my fellow participants and liked that we were in a class together.

I feel that I learned a great deal from my nightly dreams, especially that I can dive into the depths of my subcon-scious and that I am accompanied and have loving sup-port and assistance to do so. The night before I formally began my Regimen I dreamed that I met with a spiritual teacher. This teacher was a wounded healer. There was something wrong with her mouth but it did not stop her words or lessen her power as a teacher. I had been hav-ing thoughts such as, "Who am I to sign up for this proj-ect?" But the dream told me to do it. Three powerful im-ages from my dreams stay with me: planes plunging into the ocean, a wedding and sea horses guiding me into an underwater world. I am a very visual person, and these images, which have vivid meaning and associations for me, came into my consciousness frequently in waking hours.

Reading passages from Seth before sleep and also during the day was very helpful. It often seemed as if the written words were speaking directly to me and I would write down phrases that I wanted to remember. I have many pages of these phrases but one that particularly grabbed my attention was "...the sensory extravaganza that is the multidimensional existence." I want to experience that extravaganza! Another powerful phrase for me is "all imbalances may be corrected through Love and Courage." I repeat to myself that I choose Love and Courage frequently and look for ways to do so. I also think about "humility and charisma," as I know these concepts and their relationship to one another are ones that I need to work with.

Another germane concept is that of Resonance. As time passed in the 28 day period I began to feel more and more vibration in my body. Or perhaps I tuned in more and more to my interior sensations. My clue that guidance or information is available for me has always been a "tingling" which begins in my index fingers and then spreads to my hands and then to my face. Over time I began to feel that a cellular rearrangement was going on in my body. I am not always aware of what wants to be conveyed (Seth stated that help is knocking at my door and I am not answering). But I am paying greater attention to my impulses, thoughts, daydreams and am mentally throwing open that door.

Many of my impulses during the 28 days were to do something nice for myself such as get a massage, stop what I was doing and take a walk, to contact someone that I hadn't been in touch with in a long time or to attend an event that I probably wouldn't have, before paying such close attention to my impulses.

Having e-mail questions answered by Seth encouraged me that I was on the right track and the two phone sessions were especially helpful. Seth helped me to identify some fundamental aspects of my personality that are holding me back, namely lack of trust and inappropriate grief. An ongoing exploration of these issues continues to yield great benefit. Through meditation and reverie in that space between dreaming and waking I am looking at traumatic events in my early life and getting both an objectivity about them and insight into their meaning. I am beginning to wonder what it would be like to drop those barriers of self-protection and egoistic concerns. What would my body feel like? How would I move differently? How might my daily life be different? What would it feel like to meet all people and circumstances in a loving, open and fearless way? What would it be like to always have sensory access to deep joy and well being? Seth told me that I can potentially have guidance 24/7. What would that be like? I know that I can get answers to my own questions.

Negative feelings, critical or cynical thoughts and painful images would come up throughout the 28 day period. I feel that I am better at being able to step outside of myself and look at what is going on objectively. I also feel that with more practice I can make more effective use of this tool. I am remembering to put negative thoughts and images into "the box" for transformation. This practice keeps me focused on my Intent AND I really don't want to carry around such a heavy box!

And I am very curious about the transformation process going on inside. In the last few days of my regimen I came down with a serious cold. I am someone who is rarely sick and I could feel myself abruptly shutting down. Feeling miserable with a cold generated more negative thoughts to work with but I also realize that I don't want to "slam the door shut" when things get overwhelming. Adjusting to more subtle body sensations and defining my Feeling Tone requires patience and persistence, Love and Courage. I was told that I can choose to face things and not have them manifest as symptoms.

In the course of the 28 days I have been especially aware of a delight in people, people that I know and those that I see on the street, in stores, waiting rooms or gatherings. Their faces look expressive and beautiful to me. I wonder about our connections and I feel great appreciation for our individual struggles and Lessons and appreciation for what we are collectively envisioning. I think about us caring for each other and a shift in consciousness. It seems that the more I look for evidence of Love, creativity, concern for others, generosity and expansiveness, the more I see it and the more I feel it personally. Although not an entirely new sensation, I have a greater feeling of functioning in many worlds. I have made some contact with Guides and have gotten glimpses into other aspects of myself in other realities. These contacts feel tenuous but real. I have gained a greater perspective on events in my life, relationships, my profession and interests, a greater sense of connectedness to something that is ongoing and beyond the boundaries of my day to day life here in 2012. And my purpose seems clear - to awaken and live with awareness and loving responsiveness. I have come to see that my visionary goal to awaken is not a finish line to cross but rather a continuously evolving process. I am getting plenty of hints to get more playful and lighten up. I would have to laugh often that I would be attending to some mundane matter and I would suddenly hear that theme song to Mark and Seth's radio broadcast in my head and that would signal me to stop and "tune in".

Over the course of the Regimen so many positive things have happened. New patients have come to my practice. People that I have been out of touch with have contacted me. A complicated legal obligation has been resolved almost effortlessly. I have had moments of feeling so open and touched by the beauty of nature or the sweetness of being with friends. I have a new appreciation for the richness of my interior life. Even my cat seems to be off on new adventures, secret from me.

It is hard to convey in writing a process that I am just beginning to understand myself. I know that I am being assisted by Seth. He has shown me flashes of what is possible. I am convinced that the techniques that he offers lead to desired outcomes. I know that reaching my visionary goal is possible and probable. For me! The ideas in Seth's books before this project were interesting to think about, something to dream about, something that other people might have more direct access to. Now I know that this knowledge, this consciousness, is available to anyone who has the Intent and persistence to open to it. I wish the process were faster, instantaneous, but I realize that I have work to do involving Issues and Lessons.

What I really liked about having a 28 day period in which to experiment was that I could maintain a strong focus for that finite period of time. I thought about the project for large portions of each day. And night. And I think that enough understanding has come that I won't forget my goal. And I have a new Regimen in mind to begin. When I began my Regimen to awaken, I placed a small toy car, a convertible, with a heart in the driver's seat on a table in my living room. It served as a visual reminder that I was on a journey of the heart. What I have begun here continues to gather momentum. I hope that my words encourage readers to create their own Regimens that we may all contribute to an awakening world.

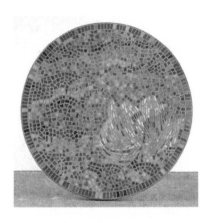

Eva in Germany

Findings of my first visionary project **2/14th to 3/13th**

If I would make a drawing for this little essay, I would take this quote of Seth "You can love your way out of this dilemma" from his and Mark's book, the next chapter in the evolution of the Soul (p. 149) in a circle and arrange the days of the project around it like a spiral. Not all of them, but most. Before I open my note book for you, I would like to describe to you how I usually start:

Each morning, it is the same ritual, I am getting up, make myself a pot of tea and then I sit down with my note-book. I begin with the sanctuary, which for me is a won-derful waterfall of golden light and love around me, next

I'm using the exercise 'the box'. What is there at the moment, what wants to be transformed, after that I am opening the chakras for the Light of All That Is, starting with the two chakras above my head to the root chakra and the connection to Grandmother Earth. This is the base line. From here I start to the dream class.

Day 1 Today it starts. I really begin at the bottom. Physical signals, limiting beliefs about myself: a feeling of unworthiness: not having a normal job, ideas for my art work vanish or are not getting finished, difficulties with my mate. It's all there.

But, this time is different. I'm writing you, Seth, and with a smile on my face. Quite typical to set up such a stage: go to the roots of all this and get a thorough reorientation. No matter what I am doing in this life, it is not the profession, which is crucial. Do I have an open heart? Am I a loving decent human being? ... What would you suggest? ...

A lightness comes, a sensation on my crown chakra, my head and the image of "my friend Harvey" comes to my mind. Okay dear, I'm giving you a push and you take a step and another push and the next step, that's how we proceed here.

Day 2 Dreams at night: The Rhine, we moved to the river, it's fantastic, our son finally has the opportunity to sail. This river looks like a lake to me. Last dream part: in a plane with a former participant of one of my classes, she, her husband and I just get on board in time, we have to run and the captain is waiting for us.

Dream class. First time we meet, that's exciting. At the end of our lesson, all of us get a little bundle with healing stones and herbs in it, very colorful. Seth, as I perceive him at the moment, looks brilliant, like the late psychologist Paul Watzlawick, he is wearing suit and tie and has an encouraging smile. This image vanishes quickly and I sense his presence more internally.

Day 3 The radio show is not on today, I feel desperate, what should I do? ... Later, there is more energy. I realize, I am the one who is sitting at the driver's wheel. My Intent is to become a visionary artist. I am going to make my first appointment with Mark and take a walk in the woods. During my walk, I discover a wooden signpost: straight man's path. For me this means straightness, clarity and insight.

Day 4 Woke up at 4:00 in the night with a quote from Martin Luther King: I have a dream! And what is my dream? Which dream is worth dreaming? ... Here is my dream worth dreaming: a dream of Peace, a dream of Harmony, a dream of Beauty. No more false lenses, but a wide and wholesome perspective. Now personalize this dream of yours. Go forward.

Day 5 Woke up with two words: Sacred Art.
During the day, I learn from one of my oldest and best friends, who just came to visit (!), that there is a possibility to study traditional art techniques in a school in London. Then, there is this man from Poland, who is conducting Earth healing rituals and Geomantie. This does not happen coincidently. Also Seth is answering my first question and I am relieved to learn that "there is no stability in terms of constant frequency. Resonance, by definition fluctuates." I feel relieved. So, it's more like inhaling, exhaling, pause. It seems, I am quite strict with myself.

Dream class: wonderful light room, I am seeing my favorite trees in front of the window. Seth is again looking like P. Watzlawick. Mark is sitting next to me and is 'giving me five' because I found my dream!

What are we doing today, Seth? He is answering me in an Austrian dialect: You are diligently knitting on your dream of Sacred Art, dear. Then pause, then you start again.

Day 6 Dream class. There is a huge sofa at the end of our class room. Seth/ P. Watzlawick just gives me a nod and I go straight to the sofa and relax. There is no pressure of achievement, leave it, put it into the box and close it. Later my teacher comes and is asking if I would dance with him, a waltz? No, not yet, I am feeling too exhausted. Okay, why don't you give me a sign? That's what I do and later we are dancing through the class room. He is greeting me with a kiss on the hand and is guiding me to my seat.

Suddenly, we are all very young maybe eight to ten years old. Okay, dream class, I want you to consciously dream your life. You already know that this life of yours is a dream. And what is our fundament? Always for the highest good of all sentient beings. Now, says Seth/ P. Watzlawick, I cannot do the work for you. Here on the shelf, you find all kinds of material to paint or making a collage or build a sculpture. Work intuitively, let your hands work by themselves.

Dreams at night: I am in a school of some sort. Many musicians are here. Am I a teacher or a student? I don't know...

Day 7 I am reading in one of Seth's books. "Your source has all the answers you need to help you manifest your heart's desire"... Then I start to change a text on a post-card from a well known artist. It says, hand written: 'Each grasp must be correct' and I am writing in my own hand: No, it doesn't have to! This is my motto.

Dream class: So again, dear, what is your dream? And I repeat my dream. Could it be a little easier for you? Simplify, you lose yourself in a net of perfection.

I have to take many attempts until I finally give up and say, I would like to be loving and kind with myself. This is accepted. You take this as your anchor, from here you start. Write it down, read it out loud, sing it...

Later that day, in my studio. What is your dream now? I would really like to find someone to share my studio. A few minutes afterwards, I get a call from a woman who found my offer in the internet. Her husband is painting and looking for a studio! (He rented it!).

Day 8 Dream class: My teacher is waiting for me. Good to see you, we have prepared a few things for you. You are able to do that on your own, we just give you another push. He is guiding me into a deep cellar/vaults. It is a mixture between a workshop and a storeroom. Here are all kind of materials and substances (stone, glass, wood, clay, plants, plastic material, tissues, threads, paper and colors). So, choose and start. I start with a prayer and intuitively I take clay and use a potter's wheel to form a Venus statue. The Venus of Willendorf (an ancient artifact, found in a cave). Afterwards I am using the shape of this figure, take plastic tissues and cut it out. Now I am having this wonderful shape of her and I am spraying this symbol on walls, streets, traffic crossings, and so on. 'Matriarchy in our time' like 'Utopia in our time' comes to my mind.

Sometime later this day, I am getting really anxious and nervous. I am having my first telephone session, I am confused about the timing and what if I cannot think of a question?

Day 9 dream class at night. Seth comes as a woman, she is wearing Greek robes, has beautiful hair and I remember this image of an Etruscan goddess, called Flora. School is over, I am alone with her and she is asking me to her desk. We are watching your efforts, all is well, you are succeeding. But don't you remember, that life itself is joyful? Wisdom and Love are not hard to achieve, you don't put it on a pedestal far away from you, you embody it and then it grows. My face gets hot, I burst out into tears, I know she is right! On the one hand I am relieved, on the other, I feel shameful. Why don't you allow yourself a look for the easy and agreeable things in your life in the second week of your regimen. Getting touched by the positive. This can be a bird singing or a spider web in the sun. Focus on receiving. Take a key word for it, write it down. What would it be? Flora and the horn of plenty. During the phone session, we touch vulnerable parts. It is all about challenging certain role models. What does it mean for me to be a wife and mother? And what is it to be an artist? To sense my true identity is the key here. I get the idea that I take a certain (critical) behavior from others as an excuse of not being the one, who I really am as a woman. In so many societies, women are far from being treated equal. Not only somewhere distant, also here in our western culture, even if it is more subtle.

Day 10 Yesterday, we also had a look at the way I was raised. 'The good girl' is rewarded and the child, who behaves like children do, is getting disciplined. A unhealthy structure, which causes a feeling of not being loved and a lack of self esteem. So, it is not about leaving and fleeing from unhealthy and limiting structures, it is all about changing and challenging from within. A different perspective.

Day 11 I didn't have conscious contact to my dream class yesterday. So much to take in, this needs time to adjust. Nurture yourself. While meditating, I get a strong sense of being in contact with a higher consciousness. An intensive feeling of warmth and being nourished.

Day 12 Dream class. Seth is constantly changing forms. From male to female, from young to old. Which form would you like? Flora would be wonderful. What is my task of today? This is for you to decide. I would love to learn more about the Etruscans. How did they live? And I am immersed in a scene of great beauty. A Southern landscape, caves, fire places.

But then, I am in front of a tipi, next to me sits a man with a wolf mask on his head. He starts talking: he is coming in human form, so that I am able to recognize him. He is wolf, I belong to the wolf clan and it is difficult for the clan, if I am not getting in contact with them. They looked out for me, it is a great gift and I am often not answering. It would be good for me to wear a necklace or so with a wolf on it.

Day 13 Dream class. No images today, main topic is to be in contact. How do I sense it? Where in my body? I would describe it as a sensation of heaviness and warmth around my head, sometimes on my shoulders, sometimes in my chest. It does feel strange at times but it is always pleasant.

Making contact doesn't always mean a literal contact in your reality. If you allow contact, you gain insight telepathically and then you start your work from there. So, there can be an inner dialogue while you are painting or making your mosaics, it just depends on your Intent and the space and freedom to do so...

Day 14 Dream at night. I am holding a speech in N.Y.C. with the title: how is every human being getting in conscious contact with his/her source.

... In my studio. I am opening a book and find an image of _____, the Egypt deity in animal form. And who is _____ for me?

Dream class. I find the hidden door to get inside, this is good. I close the door and find the other participants. We are somewhere in India, sitting under a huge tree. Seth is giving a lecture. He is signaling me that it would be better, if I continue my work, I am getting the information any way.

Back in the cellar. I am continuing with the Venus figure and suddenly I realize, she has scales like a mermaid. Which material could I use to create scales?

Day 15 Dreams at night: I am in a hospital. There is a long corridor. A physician, she is wearing a stethoscope around her neck. We are talking. Who am I, visitor, patient or a physician?

During my meditation, I am wondering, how I could get in contact with my animals and with _____, who I suppose, is another inner guide for me. Any limiting beliefs here? Parts of Roman Catholic upbringing? May be...
Also I wonder, if a further education of art therapy would be a good possibility for me to achieve my goals.

Dream class. I am not finding the class room, I am asking wolf, he runs forward and finds the door immediately. You can take a day off, if you wish, you are moving on nicely. Do you recognize that you are always in a dream? Do you recognize that dream, dream class and your life are the same, just from different perspectives? So, if anything happens to you, which is limiting you, you can always go to your dream class, an inner voice is saying.
Day 16 I am waking up with the impulse to take time outs during the day to contemplate on my divinity.

Later, I feel wobbly ... You are one of my human counterparts. You always have contact, this is ongoing. Integrate and come back to your daily routine of your morning exercises.

Day 17 Dreams at night. With a friend in London. We are walking along the road to her flat and she is really dressed up, wearing a costume, etc. But she is an artist?! Does this fit? It does. Another dream: a man in his thirties and I are going on a sailing trip, he would like to go for ten days or so, I would rather start with one or two days.

Dream class. How do I intensify the contact to my animals and inner guides? Concentrate on what you are co-creating today, what is your Intent?

Later, on my way to the studio, another inner dialogue: do you understand how life is your class? What makes you reluctant to greet this woman on the street? This is worth reflecting. Your own shadow parts, which ones? Examine... It might be the two failed marriages, this woman is facing and a strictness, I can easily sense. So these are lessons, I am also learning.

Day 18 Dreaming wide awake. Dream class: always the same setting, coming into the empty classroom, sensing my task for the moment and then I start. This time, I am meeting my 'alter ego'. He is a man in his fifties, a painter with short grey hair, having a brush in his hand. We know each other, he says, I am already doing, what you are dreaming in this moment. My heart is full of joy.

Later this day, I courageously find my way to a gallery where one artist is having her 'finissage' of her latest exhibition and is going to talk about her work process. I meet her sometimes in my dreams and I admire her way of drawing and painting.

...

Day 20 Don't worry, you are always participating, even if you don't recognize it, stay tuned in.

Day 21 This night, I sense a threat. In a store room, there are countless huge boxes in big stacksv, they are all falling down at once. I remember sanctuary, Golden light around you. This helps.

Dream class. I want you to be outside, go to your favorite place and feel your connection to all that surrounds you. Your favorite trees, the grass, the tingling of leaves. Call your animals and see, what happens. If one is coming, ask, why it came to you, get acquainted, without inner pressure.

Day 22 Dream class. Grey wolf is looking down from a roof, wiggling his tail. An idea how to remake an art work of mine, I am going to mix metal and plastic material.

Day 23 Today, I opened the website of Sethreturns and "found" three radio shows since the beginning of our project. Why didn't I do that earlier? Was this my idea of being on my own during the visionary project? I guess so. Seth's explanations and reflections about catharsis are especially valuable for me. What kind of feeling tone is separating me from my heart's dream? For me, it is a feeling of rejection and abandonment. The important task at hand is to recreate a feeling of security and being loved in this very moment. Dream class: a subtle ringing in my ears, this often happens lately when I am exploring the inner senses. Again in a cave, people are painting their bodies, they prepare for a ritual ...

Day 24 Dream class. Yosemite Park, I am standing on top of these huge rocks, inhaling the wideness of sky and landscape. I am putting all my tools and material on a blanket and start to pray. I am male now, wearing traditional clothing made of animal skin. It is a prayer of healing, healing for grandmother earth. Making art work to heal and cleanse, this would be appropriate.

Day 25 Dreams at night. My husband and I are in a meeting, again in a huge cellar with vaults. It feels good to have him around.

Dream class: I am walking along the corridor, open the door and here in the middle of the room are my sacred items. Someone is calling my Medicine name. ..., you can practice both teachings! You have two arms, two legs, you are able to work with both traditions and then integrate. ... I am taking one of my items and start to sing. For myself, for all who are with me here in this project, for grandmother earth and all sentient beings... and then, I'm falling in a deep sleep.

Day 26 What does dream class mean in its essence? An understanding to be part of the dream, of life itself. Living your life and constantly recognizing the dream within. And also, after your 28 day regimen, before you relax and connect yourself with the Divine, write down questions or remarks that come into your mind, so that I, Seth or your other inner guides can comment on it.

Day 27 Dreams at night, very lively and colorful. Traveling to the teaching. We are on a huge ship, very futuristic. I am having my bicycle with me and I am taking an elevator, but it moves from left to right instead of upside, down! An enormous movement, something is changing right here in front of my eyes.

Dream class. Again, an empty room, except an old man with white hair in a hammock, smoking a pipe. I came to make sure, you remember your dream of Peace and Harmony. He is talking in a serious manner. We are many. Explore your inner guides.

Day 28 Reaching new land of positive reality creation. It is a splendid day, nothing really happens, but all is different than usual. This is just the way it is meant to be.

During the regimen, in my waking reality, there were quite a few changes: I am experiencing a more loving relationship to my husband, a more positive look on daily routine in general and I accomplished a mosaic art work which I had planned for almost a year. I am also very pleased that I am sharing my studio now. New topics for the next project are there and want to be looked at.

The highest
good for
all concerned...

Charmaine in New Zealand

My goal for the regimen was:
I will shed my sense of inferiority and lack of self worth,
and walk into self belief and my personal power.

The techniques I proposed to use to support this were:
Distracting the ego
The metaphorical tools
Calling in my guides
The box
Embodying the opposite
Suspending disbelief
Consecutive positive assessments

Before I began the regimen, I personalized the techniques
so that they became easily accessible when in need:

To distract the ego, I used a couple of mantras that effectively tuned me into another wavelength - "The highest good for all concerned"; Seth predicting "a quantum leap of understanding before the end of the project."

The metaphorical tool I used was slipping into a "suit of personal power," an ethereal fitted glove that became like powerful armour.

The box - I saw this like a spa sanctuary for unwanted thoughts and emotions - a serene washing machine

Embodying the opposite - encouraging a memory of being welcomed into a huge family of friends.

Suspending disbelief - reminding myself that "miracles happen everywhere," and there is a "great probability that I will get what I wish for sooner rather than later."

Consecutive Positive Assessments - trying to recapture the blissful, unencumbered memories from meditation.

I initially thought I would keep a daily count of how often each of these were used, but found that on most days, I used these techniques often.

At the centre of my issue was how I allow other people to treat me (especially in my work place) and secondly how I handle being in a large group of people (especially when I might be called upon to speak publicly.) (Most days generally roll easily, but my problem lies when I am confronted/challenged/negated in some way, and I can not defend myself.)

I started my regimen full of enthusiasm and anticipation. I had already used several techniques successfully at various times on other goals, so I was somewhat familiar with some of them. Many impulses came to me spontaneously during the days - sometimes I had no way of writing things down, and they may have been lost. Other times I would recite them in my head to make sure I wrote them down when I could. I have added them in places where they related to at the time.

My Findings

Each morning I would start my day with up to one hour's meditation. I have now reached a stage where this would set the scene for the day. I became able to disassociate myself from the mundane things in my life quite well. I would generally leave the house each morning in a calm blissful state, not feeling assertive or domineering, but rather unaffected and remote, unworried, disconnected even, just going about my business without the usual dread or wishing I was somewhere else. On re-reading my journal, I found many passages stating things like "I feel calm and detached," "I am unworried about work pressure."

Impulse: when you are on the divine plane, thinking for the greater good of all, you don't actually have to deal with things that go wrong, or devise strategies for people who attack you, because those things don't actually happen. (i.e. it's not that you better deal with them or better deflect them, it's that they DON'T ARISE).

Each morning I would request the name of my Energy Personality or Guide. I would also ask for some contact - visual, physical, emotional etc. Early on I received the name 'Gilda'. It came without real effort - just popped into my mind. This name had been given to me about six months ago but I hadn't done anything with it. Now it resurfaced, and I felt it was too much of a coincidence for me to be making it up. Over the Regimen I tried to communicate often, but have not felt a lot of connection. I tried to talk, ask questions etc, but have not felt any real presence. This has remained the same I think for the 28 days.

As most days wore on, some of the early morning euphoria wore off. I would find that I would have to consciously employ some of the techniques to regain the calmness, and steer away from the negativity.

The repeated mantra 'the highest good for all concerned' would immediately realign my thinking. It was like the meaning contained far more than what the words stated. I would suddenly be reminded of a huge truth. I could turn around my thoughts quickly.

One of the most successful early techniques was using the metaphorical tool of my personal suit of power. It fitted externally and internally and sort of sucked into myself. I repeatedly walked into this and there was satisfaction of being attached to my personal power. This was an exciting feeling - like putting a mask on and becoming someone other than myself - or perhaps another version of myself. Maybe it should have been approached from another angle - like discarding a layer, thereby dropping the 'habit'. I would easily envision this to bolster myself when I felt my energy ebbing away.

Distracting the ego became really valuable further into the Regimen. I would find myself playing out stupid scenarios in my head - and it was on the auto-repeat setting.

It was such a wrench to drag myself away from this, and I was not always successful.

When things got challenging during the Regimen, I would use many of the techniques all at once. I would recklessly go from one technique to another, to see if I could pull myself away from the drama. On one occasion I called in everyone I could think of (including Seth) and asked for Love and assistance. I was able to fully turn around my feeling of inferiority and being bullied, and was able to remain in a peaceful vibration. I did have to work hard at pulling myself away from one reality to another - when things are uncomfortable, it is much harder to tune out.

It came to me after about a week, however, that I was not having to employ the techniques all the time, as I no longer had the nervous defensive chatter running through my head. On quite a few occasions in my journal I have written "am able to remain in this tranquil state. It's like a cocoon. I feel one step removed. Am still playing episodes of powerless in my head, but would have to say they lack the sting that they held previously."; "hasn't got the same urgency"; "when I am in a state of uplifted awareness and feel unprovoked by my issues, I don't think of them as solved, rather I don't think of them as issues at all. It's almost as if they don't or have never existed." I am not seeing myself as powerless, or the contrary as powerful.

Some days, right from the start, I was more involved in the mundane and less in the Divine. I tried to recall the space I had previously been in, but would get too involved in the incessant chatter in my head. It came to me that even small awakened moments are of value.

Listening to the Seth's talks on the Visionary Project were valuable. I also found that reading articles from various complementary websites about the coming Shift and ascension were like having a dose of inspiration. It was like much needed encouragement at the end of the day from the coach!

During the regimen, I did have the expectation that there would be a major shift and that a lot would be cleared. I was working diligently with the techniques and seemingly had things under control and making progress toward my goal. I had not tested my new found confidence in a larger group situation, so realized I had neglected part of the equation. When I tried to experience my progress in a Trance state, I still felt the anxiety that came with encountering groups of people, although this was perhaps not so pronounced. I was reminded to employ the techniques in earnest around this.

Impulse: I am trying to live up to an idealized version of me.

Throughout the regimen I had no recall of the dream classroom. Each night as instructed, I would read a passage from Seth's works which inspired me. I chose "The denial of ones own power does serve in the learning of lessons, for example. If you are here to become powerful, then, the initial denial of your own power to create gives you something to motivate your awakening... Then, as if by a miracle, your questions are answered in a Moment of Awakening one morning." (2012 and Beyond, pg 6-7). It completely sums up where I am, and the outcome is so perfect. It immediately fills me with such hope. I found it very empowering. However, it did not bring me any closer to remembering anything of the actual dream classroom. The lessons however may have been transmitted as the many impulses I received.

Approximately half way through the Regimen, I encountered a situation that reminded me just how flimsy my progress was (or so it seemed). I began to consider that it was not enough to just employ the techniques, and wondered whether they were just masking the actual issue. I felt like I was not considering the whole. There were repeated niggles that the techniques were not going to be wholly the answer.

This became the basis of my first question to Seth - does the original catalyst for my lack of personal power need to be unearthed. I asked Seth if I needed to go back and discover all the traumatic episodes that make me fearful of people, resulting in lack of self-esteem. Seth did indeed respond that this was what needed to be done, and he went over the techniques I might use to have this revealed.

I then endeavoured to unblock the memories that were keeping the old habits in place. I tried many short Trances to see what transpired, and also tried during my meditation in the morning. I understood that this would be repetitious work. I would have to describe the process as very saddening. I felt very out of my depth. I tried not to feel emotionally involved, but it was hard just to be the observer. I would not say this was really successful. I didn't feel I unearthed anything that I had not got on many previous attempts. I didn't feel greatly connected to the child - I felt empathic with the situation, but not very connected.

Impulse: Huge positive effects have already occurred - don't be disheartened.

Impulse: I don't have to achieve huge miracles, although miracles will occur.

Impulse: I got that it is my 'voice' that had been stifled - was not to be heard.

Impulse: don't have to keep rationalizing my 'issues', just acknowledge them without judgment.

I did become fearful that if I didn't get to grips with this issue, that I may not ascend into the 4th Dimension. What if I couldn't get this done?

Since then, there has been an overwhelming urge to uncover the hidden past. Seth said the most difficult parts would be the most reluctant to surface. It has really plagued me. And to seemingly stress the importance of unraveling the issue, I have had encounters at work that have really pushed me to the extreme. I understand that this is being created by me, but at times I have felt at the end of my tether. If I do not sort this out, my complete recovery will not occur. It is pushing for me to find it, and I am very preoccupied. Now it is difficult to revert to the blissful state, and I remain agitated. Distracting the ego proves difficult. It's almost like I could over-ride the anxiety and step back, but to do this would mean the root of the issue would remain undisclosed, and would still need to be dealt with at some stage. I have implored my Guides to help, but they remain quiet. I am desperate to engage my Energy Personality more.

With all this going on, I do have to report that there have been many inspiring impulses being sent through to me. It is a wonderful thing.

Impulse: Life is a game, it is 'reworked' on a nightly basis when my consciousness is asleep. So in theory, each day could be very different. Any issue could just dissolve "like that!" I had considerable success with this catch-phrase - life is a game. It reminded me that everything is set up by ourselves. This was very distracting and good for me!

At times of quiet, I am aware of my soul presence just below the surface, reminding me I am supported.

Impulse: This is an on-going project, it does not have to have a perfect outcome. Progress is progress - stop expecting too much. Keep to the Regimen.

Impulse: Keep revising the things uncovered in my past - more will be revealed. It will serve as a catalyst to getting more of the nitty gritty.

Impulse: The dreary feeling I have now I have because I am hoping to have a 'complete cure' within these 28 days, and there is so much fear and pressure around not being able to achieve this.

At the end of the 28 days, I would have to say that I remain unable to unlock the hidden childhood memory. I am going to let it settle perhaps - although it may well push further for release. I don't feel I want to repress it again, as it will always be impeding my awakening - always on the periphery.

In conclusion, I will continue with the Regimen. I think once I have reported my Findings I will feel relieved. Just writing this report has enabled me to recapture and remember some of the wonderful benefits that have accrued, and I know that all is not insurmountable. EVEN THE NEGATIVE THINGS ARE POSITIVES AS WELL. It has given me resolve to retry things and not expect a perfect outcome straight away. I shall continue where I left off.

Shelton in Italy

My Notes to the Over Soul.

My objectives:

Higher Consciousness (the raising of spiritual vibration)

An Improved Reality Creation Towards Value Fulfillment (co-creating consciously)

To Meet An Awakened Soul Group or Mentor in the Study of Metaphysics (strength in numbers)

My foundational precepts:

"You create your own reality."

"Emotion is the creative energy of All That Is in action."

"Your intention, emotions and beliefs provide the energy and direction for reality creation."

"Everything exists initially as gestalts of consciousness, the non physical templates of creation."

133

The Box

I visualize a dark grey 4x4 metal box, all 4 sides have the Celtic symbol representing the tripartite energies. It's the symbol Mark used for his trilogy books. When using the box technique I visualize myself walking towards the box with my issue in hand and from the corner of my eye I can see the shape of a shadowy muscular figure sliding it open for me then slams it shut once the item is in. At that point the entire box illuminates with a bright silver light which highlights the Celtic symbol and in a few seconds all fades to black. I tell you that it works every time and I wasn't aware of the content transformation until Seth made mention during the "ending and beginnings" radio show. Whatever is placed in the box "will" soften until it transforms into a positive, but that accomplishment will request your highest desire and faith for it to happen.

Daily Habitual Use of:
Consecutive Positive Assessments
Suspending Disbelief
Reading the Emotional Body
Belief Revision
Healing Talk

2-11-2012

Today I experimented with catching my habitual conversations (negative minions) by using the Moment Point. I seized the "moment" to change my thoughts with dialogue towards a positive discussion. When I embody the precept "You create your own reality," it gives me that extra courage. I'm 100% responsible for which way my creation goes. Reconfiguring negative habitual thoughts produces a quick rise and softening of the emotions.

2-12-2012

Today I'm noticing how much determination and discipline is needed to maintain an awakened state. I can see that my regimen started weeks before the class began. I feel at home using Seth's metaphysical tools. Today my Lesson was about reinforcing the positive feelings within me. The word for the day is "self empowerment."

2-13-2012

I received a message after awakening from the dream state this morning about loving energies. I didn't remember to use this advice and learned a valuable lesson. Today was about learning how to observe life's little dramas without a scornful eye and getting accustomed to nurturing "Patience" within myself. Tricky tricky tricky.

2-14-2012

I dreamt of repairing Leather seats. Go figure...

I have feelings of giddiness and loving energies. I am mentally incorporating the "Divine Day" regimen with the CPA technique to acknowledge and give thanks (co-creating). I am embodying the idea of consciously "fueling the positive" within each moment. Each Moment Point that I claim as my own extends the impulse and gives it back at the same time.

Lesson: co-creating with loving energies.

2-15-2012

I am extending the Divine Day regimen again because it feels good and it works. As I build confidence believing in a Divine Day my focus is sharpening. When I take the advice from my intuitive nudging regarding a course of action, the day becomes effortless as if "time" is speeding up. My Lesson today dealt with grounding and raising the momentum of positive feelings. The idea of "extending positive energy" must be embodied fully for the effects to heighten and gain force.

"The best place to be is Being".

2-16-2012

Toying with random images, faces or places that pop in and out of my awareness: the idea that these impulses are a sneak preview to the events with such persons or places in my near future. So there is a lag time to turn any visual impulse into a divine event in the future as long as I "remember" that these visual impulses are sign posts. They could be negative images or positive ones, but when they do pop in, grab em! Then I mix a little courage and loving understanding and change the scene so they feel "good to the last drop." I call this "imprinting" or "copywriting" a positive scene within my mental landscape. I do this often enough that what I wish to think or watch on the screen of my mind is a beautiful picture. Easier said than done.

2-17-2012

I'm on a roll and gaining momentum. Noticing how the previous weeks of creating a blueprint out of the Precepts and applying them to my everyday life has solidified into a working model that I can consciously navigate. I am much more excited than before to push this a step further and not deny myself an extended sip from the divine. I'm feeling elated today.

2-19-2012

Focused on the inner self and kept a stream of calm for most of the day until a lesson or two rears its head. This happens often when things are on the upstream. I'm stretching the moment for longer periods of time as effortlessly as possible and just sitting within that space where monkey-mind chatter does not exist. I notice the dance between the ego and heart's desire because they both vie for my attention. It takes less than a fraction of a second to either learn a lesson or create a blessing. You're right Seth, it does take courage and loving understanding "in the moment:" the courage not to react, the love to smooth things over and the understanding of what your intentions truly are.

2-20-2012

Consciousness was my theme. I spent most of my waking hours in the uncommon trance. I am moving further within the spacious moment of mentally\ physically "Being." As I do, my daily activities take on an airy feel as if I'm standing right here and by the same token I'm not. I feel this "disconnect" because my senses are moving towards other activities leaving only my intuition as my guide. This experience reminds me of a scene from the movie The Matrix where Morpheus takes Neo for the first time to the construct which represented a computer generated empty space where you gather, access and download further knowledge for the journey ahead.

2-21-2012

"BAM", Fear, worry and discomforting feelings nearly knocking the wind out of me today, but I'm not surprised at how quickly they tapered off. Fear has no place the more I walk within the uncommon trance. Divine consciousness becomes my new co-pilot. The four precepts that I currently use are paramount in developing self-empowerment and releasing fear. At times I feel a physical sensation of lightness ushering me in a uniform direction. Depending on my state of Being, this impulse is my beacon home. I wouldn't be able to identify this if it wasn't for my Conscious effort in using the four precepts.

"It is only the voices from within you that make it difficult."

2-22-2012

Today's findings are an extension from previous days regarding the uncommon trance. This is where the magic happens. Depending on my bent of mind during the day I experience sensations of feeling taller than usual. This happens when my appreciation for the moment point deepens. The moment point for me is a moment to actually feel my way through any situation that presents itself. This embodiment makes it easier to "let go" of anything contrary to my soul's evolution.

"To walk the uncommon trance is a constant reminder to stay focused on all or any precepts necessary".

3-4-2012

From Feb. 23 - March 3 a total of 9 days of heartfelt written work was deleted! Deleted by the impatient side of me doing tasks at a fast pace "without thinking?" Losing my data stirred up some feelings as you can imagine. I stopped in my tracks, took a deep breath and as I stood silent the still voice within nudged and had this to say:

"Much was covered during this period and that will not be lost, the application of the techniques are evident in your waking world and much was gained. There's no "time" left for guessing because the blue print to our souls evolution towards value fulfillment is under way, the completion in the lack of faith is at hand and old beliefs tightly held are changing. This is the beginning of a new adventure which requests conscious participation during this time of harvest, the gate way is open, promises were kept, it's time to head home".
What a thought huh?

3-5-2012

This Awakening is quickening. I am so relieved that my mental stability is no longer overshadowed with uncertainty. In the uncommon trance any negative feeling or thought can be replaced automatically with its opposite and the results are a sense of assurance, stability and a calm demeanor. Within this state I can hear a soft ringing in my ears as you would experience when wearing ear plugs. It's like a homing signal for me. Btw, I do have normal checkups so my hearing is just fine in case you were wondering. :)

3-6-2012
Today was a test of my conviction towards maintaining mental equilibrium. I dealt with bouts of uneasiness and insecure emotions, a bleed through maybe, from a simultaneous me going through the emotions, because I'm minding my own business and feeling just fantastic! Or could it be residue coming up for a little clearing? Tonight as I write this entry I can sense the "something must be wrong" feelings brewing. These feelings of impending doom pop up whenever good things are beginning to surface. When this feeling surfaces it's as if a part of me doesn't believe that "goodness" is our birthright. "Healing" is an ongoing process, so as I ride the wave of spiritual ecstasy while sipping a "divine" cocktail that is the time to observe the inner sway. The distractions I face in waking life vary from day to day so I take great care to be mindful of my inner sway. My remedy is CPA,

as a reminder that the Abundant Universe is right there in front of me and there is absolutely nothing to fear!

"Instead of attributing these uneasy feelings specifically to negative events, begin to see the events as a reflection of what is coalescing within the self".

3-7-2012

I am at the tail end of a 24 hr negativity bug. A sense of groundedness is returning. What a release from the tension that was building but more important is how quickly these bouts of negativity fade. I've noticed how these types of feelings replay themselves over and over again masquerading under many guises. But it is a test, a spiritual test for my soul's evolution. So I decided today to recognize my little minions of negativity and bless each of them for helping me to spiritually mature. Now the real trick is finding the others that operate in silent running. Patience, patience, patience is a virtue worth the value because we're in for the long haul!

There's a part of me that feels naked without the old beliefs because they were a custom fit and I knew of no other way to live. But today is different. I am becoming a metaphysical stylist of sorts weaving the fabric of life into a beautiful new robe and I shall wear it well.

3-9-2012

Today I am vibrating at a higher frequency and I recognize the difference in myself when I look into my eyes in the mirror. I can feel the underlying stream of positive energy quite freely. I learned how to tweak it to a degree. The 28 day experiment was/is a success and I'm very pleased with my discoveries and in no way is this the final stage of the play but an ongoing "work in progress." As a student of consciousness I had a glimpse of what a co-creator can achieve. I am on constant patrol of my mental mansion, ripping down walls and opening darkened pathways that denied access to other areas of consciousness.

We are in a time of great power to become all we desire to be. There is no one person or thing standing in our way to success. We must be like the children. You see how they play? They play and live life in a "Divine" way.

Ritual of Sanctuary

The Ritual of Sanctuary was presented to readers in our book on *Soul Evolution* when we first began to emphasize direct exploration of the Unknown Reality. We felt that the reader would require some personalized protection in their experimentation.

The most simple form of the Ritual is to imagine, prior to psychic pursuits, a golden Light surrounding you. Nothing harmful can penetrate this field of Light. It has a healing protective influence. You may certainly use this simplified form while you go about creating your own Ritual.

The object here is to generate positive energies with your creative consciousness. Try listing on a piece of paper your positive beliefs and ideas that denote security, peace, and protection. The next step would be, perhaps artistically, to distill these potent concepts down into an image, statement, or physical object that Resonates with the protective energies. Naturally you may include gestures, visualizations, or any other evocative materials.

Practice your Ritual until you can create at-will the state of Sanctuary within your own consciousness. Only you will know when you are successful.

Glossary

Definitions for the concepts Seth discusses in this book.

All That Is - The energy source from which all life sprung throughout the multitude of Universes, transcending all dimensions of consciousness and being part of all. Also referred to as the Logos and Evolutionary Consciousness.

Altared States - Ritualizing and making sacred the mundane activities of existence creates elevated states of consciousness.

Ancient Wisdom - The knowledge of the magicians, shamans, witches and healers of the past.

Awakening - As the Ancient Wisdom is remembered by humanity, an awareness of the greater reality is experienced by individuals.

Beliefs - Ideas, images, and emotions within your mental environment that act as filters and norms in the creation of Personal Realities.

Bleedthroughs - Momentary experiencing of lives being lived in other tirmeframes and other systems of reality.

Catharsis - Recovering lost aspects of the Essential Identity.

Co-creation - You co-create your reality with the limitless creative energies of All That Is.

Consciousness Units (CU's) - The theorized building blocks of realities. Elements of awarized energy that are telepathic and holographic.

Courage - Courage and Loving Understanding replace fear and anger in the creation of Positive Realities.

Denial - The ego/intellect prevents the learning of Lessons by denying the truth of the matter.

Dimensions - Points of reference from one reality to the other with different vibrational wavelengths of consciousness.

Divine Day - The student attempts to live a complete waking day while maintaining contact with the Energy Personality.

Divine Will - The will is potentiated through ongoing contact and communication with Beings of Light. Also called Intent.

Ego/Intellect - The aspect of the personality that attempts to maintain the status quo reality.

Ecstasy - The positive emotion experienced in contact with the Divine.

Embodiment - Precepts are lived in the creation of improved realities.

Energy Personality - A being capable of transferring their thought energy inter-dimensionally to physical beings and sometimes using the physical abilities of those beings for communication.

Glossary

Entity - Being not presently manifested on the physical plane. Also known as a Spirit.

Essential Identity - A truthful representation of the personality as perceived with the Inner Senses.

Feeling-Tone - Thoughts, images, sounds and assorted sensory data that represent a particular state of consciousness, event, or existence.

Fourth-Dimensional Shift - Consciousness expands as the individual experiences an awareness of all Simultaneous Existences. Also called Unity of Consciousness Awareness.

Gestalts of Consciousness - Assemblages of Consciousness Units into Reality Constructs of all types.

gods - Consciousness personalized and projected outward into reality. A self-created projection of the developing ego.

Holographic Insert - Teaching aid of the non-physical beings. Multisensory construct experienced with the Inner Senses.

Incarnation - To move oneself into another life experience on the physical plane.

Inner Sense - The Soul's perspective. Both the creator and the perceiver of Personal Realities.

Intellectualization - The aspect of the psyche that attempts to figure things out so that the status quo is maintained.

Intention - See Divine Will.

Lessons - Chosen life experiences of the Soul for further spiritual evolution.

Light Body - The etheric body of refined light.

Love - Love with a capital L is the force behind manifestation in the Third Dimension.

Moment Point - The current empowered moment of awakening. Exists as a portal to all points past, present and future and all Simultaneous Lives.

Mystery Civilizations - Foundational civilizations largely unknown to modern science. Some examples are Atlantis, Lemuria and GA.

Negative Emotion - Habitual creation of negative emotions creates enduring negative realities.

Negative Entities - Negative energies that roam the Universes in pursuit of their own power to dominate.

Negative Persona - Rejected and repressed aspects of the personal identity.

Percept - Perception creates reality in the Third Dimension through the Inner Senses.

Personal Reality Field - The radius within your self created world within which you have the most control in the creation of Reality Constructs.

Precept - Empowered concepts of manifestation. Example: you create your own reality.

Reality - That which one assumes to be true based on one's thoughts and experiences. Also called Perceived Reality.

Reality Creation - Consciousness creates reality.

Reincarnational Drama - Soul Family drama enacted to teach the participants a Lesson in Value Fulfillment.

Scientist of Consciousness - The researcher studies the phenomena within the Personal Reality Field by testing hypotheses in experimentation. See Precept.

Observer Perspective - Self-created aspect of consciousness that sees beyond the limitations of the ego/intellect. An intermediary position between the ego and the Soul Self.

Seth - An energy personality essence that has appeared within the mental environments of humans throughout the millennia to educate and inspire.

Simultaneous Lives - The multidimensional simultaneous experiences of Souls in incarnation.

Soul - The non-physical counterpart to the physical human body, personality, and mentality. The spiritual aspect of the human.

Soul Evolution - The conscious learning of Lessons without denial or intellectualization.

Soul Family - The group of humans you incarnate with lifetime after lifetime to learn your Lessons together.

Spiritual Hierarchy - Beings of Light who have mastered multidimensional levels of experience throughout the Universes and have moved on to higher service in the evolution of all Souls.

The Christ - The embodiment of The Christ in your World. Also called World Teacher. First described in Seth Speaks.

The Council - Members of the Spiritual Hierarchy. Highly evolved beings that advise Souls on incarnations for their spiritual evolution.

The New World - The Positive Manifestation

The Vanguard - Advocates for humanity and Mother Earth who incarnate together to lead progressive movements of various kinds.

Third Dimension - The physical plane of Earthly existence.

Trance State - The relaxed, focused state of awareness that allows the Scientist of Consciousness to conduct experiments and collect data.

Value Fulfillment - Consciousness seeks manifestation of itself into all realities via the fulfillment of all values.

Visionary - Reincarnated magicians, shamans, witches and healers in this current timeframe.

I think we're going to have to do a book or two or three
or four or many more to get the masses
to see the problem ... Seth

MORE BOOKS?

Seth has promised to continue to communicate with us
to further the awakening of humanity. This means that
there will be an ongoing source of current, inspirational
messages available from: **Seth Returns Publishing**

Communications from Seth
on the Awakening of Humanity
9/11: The Unknown Reality of the World
The first original Seth book in two decades
The Next Chapter in the Evolution of the Soul
The Scientist of Consciousness Workbook
Thought Reality
The Healing Regimen and Spiritual Prosperity

The Trilogy
All That Is - Seth Comments on the Creative Source
Mystery Civilizations - Seth Answers Reader's
Questions on Legendary Civilizations
Soul Mate/Soul Family - Contains the Soul Mate
Project

Seth - A Multidimensional Autobiography
Resonance - Manifesting Your Heart's Desire
Love Being - Waking Up in the New Consciousness

Order the new Seth books at your local book-
store or through amazon worldwide.

CPSIA information can be obtained at www.ICGtesting.com
Printed in the USA
BVOW07s2158250614

357273BV00002B/4/P